Seasons

Seasons

FROM
The Whole Year Round

BY
Dallas Lore Sharp

WITH ILLUSTRATIONS BY
Robert Bruce Horsfall

Republished by the South Jersey Culture & History Center
2014

This edition published 2014 by South Jersey Culture & History
Center

South Jersey Culture & History Center, The Richard Stockton
College of New Jersey, 101 Vera King Farris Drive, Galloway,
New Jersey, 08205

Title: Seasons
Author: Sharp, Dallas Lore

ISBN: 978-0-9888731-1-7

Contents

Foreword to New Edition

"When April wind makes the call of the soil, I hold the plough as my only hold upon the earth, and, as I follow through the fresh and fragrant furrow, I am planted with every footstep, growing, budding, blooming in a spirit of spring."

The Hills of Hingham

The greatest revelations about the nature of life and of humanity are often found in the smallest venues, overlooked and unremarked upon. It is the rare and honest soul that can find meaning in the mundane. Dallas Lore Sharp (1870-1929), naturalist, academic and author, possessed such a soul.

Sharp was born on December 13, 1870, in Haleyville, Cumberland County, New Jersey. His youth was spent in the fields, forests, and swamps of South Jersey, exploring the Cohansey and Back Creeks, the Maurice River, and Bear Swamp. He graduated from Brown University in 1895, the same year he was ordained as a minister in the Methodist Episcopal church. He received a degree in theology from Boston University in 1899, but pursued a secular career, first as librarian at Boston University and eventually as Professor of English.

Among the most popular nature writers of his time, Sharp wrote essays and field guides for popular magazines such as the *Atlantic Monthly* and several book-length collections, some which sold over 100,000 copies. He mused on the aspects of nature that could be found in one's backyard: native birds, small mammals, creeks and trees and loose fall leaves. He successfully translated the wild world into his readers' living rooms.

Writing of his youth in South Jersey as well as his adult life in Massachusetts, Sharp reveals a view of nature that is nearly mystical. Although his is a nature not always accessed by the average individual, it *is* accessible. Sharp often points his work directly at the young, and expends his efforts to educate them about the glories of the untamed nature within their back yards and beyond, over the fences and into the fields and forests.

The present volume is a selection of essays from *The Whole Year Round*, originally published as four shorter texts, each based on a season. In these essays Sharp concentrates upon the small scale of the world: flora and fauna in back yard and pasture, pines, bees, muskrat and geese. Focus on the small serves to highlight the grandness of nature as a whole. As an avid conservationist — though one of his day, to be sure — he urged readers to become involved in stewardship of the world around them.

As a married man with four sons, Sharp gave readers a window into his own life, personalizing his views as naturalist and inviting readers to experience the world as he and his family experienced it — as a long series of pleasurable moments, both quiet and rambunctious, intertwining humanity with the many creatures of nature.

The appeal of Sharp's work is not that he writes about the Seven Wonders, the Grand Canyon or Niagara Falls. Neither does he provide a scientific treatise on the natural world. Rather, he presents the view of a man raised from youth to enjoy deeply the adventure of subdued pastures, changing seasons, and the natural world surrounding us all. His idealized visions of forests, fields and streams were written for an audience who found themselves in increasingly urban environments. Look, he says, to city and country dwellers alike, there are small wonders to be found all around. *The Independent*, reviewing Sharp's 1916 work *The Hills of Hingham*, wrote, "He loves hills and bees and open fires. He has a sense of words, a sense of humor and a sense of the infinite. He writes with charm and sincerity of the little things of life, and of the big things." That is just the appeal of Sharp's works, particularly in the case of *The Whole Year Round*. His essays address philosophy by way of flowers and winter birds. With open eyes and dry wit, Sharp discusses the role that nature can play in our lives, and the role we can play toward it.

Like the nature he describes, Sharp's work amply repays attentive reading. Crafted with lovely, understated skill, these essays entertain with a purpose that Sharp summarized thusly in *The Fall of the Year* : "This is a divinely beautiful world, a marvelously interesting world, the best conceivable sort of a world to live in, notwithstanding its gypsy moths, tornadoes, and germs, its laws of gravity, and of cause and effect; and my purpose . . . is to help my readers to come by this belief."

Renee Fern

Galloway Township, 2014

INTRODUCTION

The writer of this book has four children of his own, and not so very long ago (he can remember it) he was a child himself, and roamed the fields, as still he does, with all the child's love of freedom and joy in the companionship of wild things — wild lives, wild winds, wild places, and the wild hours along the edge of dusk and dawn. And if he has any right to ask other children than his own to tramp the wild places with him through the pages of this book it is because he is still a child and cannot outgrow his love of Saturdays and skates and deep woods and the ways of the wild folk, great and small; and because, again, he has tramped the wild places (for his home is in the woods) more than most of his readers, perhaps, and tramped them the seasons round — stormy nights and lazy autumn days, and summer and winter; and he has seen — only what his readers have seen, no doubt, — the ordinary things, but he has often felt, as all children do at times feel, strange deep things, things more wonderful than anybody ever saw. And yet the ordinary things, ordinary only because we have not watched them and thought about them, are really what we are going out to see; and we are going out in an ordinary way — upon our two feet, barefoot when we can, in rubber boots if we must; sometimes with a fish-pole, sometimes with a hoe; sometimes with a camera — but never with a gun; and if we see nothing more than the sky and the earth, we shall not have had our tramp in vain — not if the sky is full of clouds or storm or stars; and not if the earth is full of wideness and freshness and freedom; and not if our hearts are full of — it may be, of those strange deep feelings that the hearts of children know.

And so the author hopes that this book in its new cover, with its new name (it is made of four books of the seasons bound in one) will find its way into many homes, where the four separate books went only to the schools. And if it comes to your home, he hopes that it will take you into the fields and woods and, if possible, cause you to love them and all their wilding life more.

Dallas Lore Sharp
Mullein Hill, 1914

THE SEASON OF
SPRING

AN OLD APPLE TREE

Beyond the meadow, perhaps half a mile from my window, stands an old apple tree, the last of an ancient line that once marked the boundary between the "upper" and the "lower" pastures. It is a bent, broken, hoary old tree, grizzled with suckers from feet to crown. No one has pruned it for half a century; no one ever gathers its gnarly apples — no one but the cattle who love to lie in its shadow and munch its fruit.

The cows know the tree. One of their winding paths runs under its low-hung branches; and as I frequently travel the cow-paths, I also find my way thither. Yet I do not go for apples, nor just because the cow-path takes me. That old apple tree is hollow, hollow all over, trunk and branches, as hollow as a lodging-house; and I have never known it when it was not "putting up" some wayfaring visitor or some permanent lodger. So I go over, whenever I have a chance, to call upon my friends or pay my respects to the distinguished guests. This old tree is on the neighboring farm. It does not belong to me, and I am glad; for if it did, then I should have to trim it, and scrape it, and plaster up its holes, and put a burlap petticoat on it, all because of the gruesome gypsy moths that infest my trees. Oh, yes, that would make it bear better apples, but what then would become of its birds and beasts? Everybody ought to have *one* apple tree that bears birds and beasts — and Baldwin apples, too, of course, if the three sorts of fruit can be made to grow on the same tree. But only the birds and beasts grow well on the untrimmed,

13

unscraped, unplastered, unpetticoated old tree yonder between the pastures. His heart is wide open to every small traveler passing by.

Whenever I look over toward the old tree, I think of the old vine-covered, weather-beaten house in which my grandfather lived, where many a traveler put up over night — to get a plate of grandmother's buckwheat cakes, I think, and a taste of her keen wit. The old house sat in under a grove of pin oak and pine, — "Underwood" we called it, — a sheltered, sheltering spot; with a peddler's stall in the barn, a peddler's place at the table, a peddler's bed in the herby garret, a boundless, fathomless featherbed, of a piece with the house and the hospitality. There were larger houses and newer, in the neighborhood; but no other house in all the region, not even the tavern, two miles farther down the pike, was half so central, or so homelike, or so full of sweet and juicy gossip. The old apple tree yonder between the woods and the meadow is as central, as hospitable, and, if animals talk with one another, just as full of neighborhood news as was grandfather's roof-tree.

Of course you would never suspect it, passing by. But then, no lover of wild things passes by — never without first stopping, and especially before an old tree all full of holes. Whenever you see a hole in a tree, in a sand-bank, in a hillside, under a rail-pile — anywhere out of doors, stop!

Stop here beside this decrepit apple tree. No, you will find no sign swinging from the front, no doorplate, no letter-box bearing the name of the family residing here. The birds and beasts do not advertise their houses so. They would hide their houses, they would have you pass by; for most persons are rude in the woods and fields, breaking into the homes of the wood-folk as they never would dream of doing in the case of their human neighbors.

There is no need of being rude anywhere, no need of being an unwelcome visitor even to the shyest and most timid of the little people of the fields. Come over with me — they know me in the old apple tree. It is nearly sundown. The evening is near, with night at its heels, for it is an early March day.

We shall not wait long. The doors will open that we may enter — enter into a home of the fields, and, a little way at least, into a life of the fields, for, as I have said, this old tree has a small dweller of some sort the year round.

On this March day we shall be admitted by my owls. They take possession late in winter and occupy the tree, with some curious fellow tenants, until early summer. I can count upon these small screech owls by February, — the forlorn month, the seasonless, hopeless, lifeless month of the year, but for its owls, its thaws, its lengthening days, its cackling pullets, its possible bluebirds, and its being the year's end! At least the ancients called February, not December, the year's end, maintaining, with some sense, that the making of the world was begun in March, that is, with the spring. The owls do not, like the swallows, bring the spring, but they nevertheless help winter with most seemly haste into an early grave.

If, as the dusk comes down, I cannot go over to the tree, I will go to my window and watch. I cannot see him, the grim-beaked baron with his hooked talons, his ghostly wings, his night-seeing eyes, but I know that he has come to his window in the apple-tree turret yonder against the darkening sky, and that he watches with me. I cannot see him swoop downward over the ditches, nor see him quarter the meadow, beating, dangling, dropping between the flattened tussocks; nor can I hear him, as, back on the silent shadows, he slants upward again to his tower. Mine are human eyes, human ears. Even the quick-eared meadow mouse did not hear until the long talons closed and it was too late.

But there have been times when, like some belated traveler, I have been forced to cross this wild nightland of his; and I have *felt* him pass — so near at times that he has stirred my hair, by the wind — dare I say? — of his mysterious wings. At other times I have heard him. Often on the edge of night I have listened to his quavering, querulous cry from the elm-tops below me by the meadow. But oftener I have watched at the casement here in my castle wall.

Away yonder on the borders of night, dim and gloomy, looms his ancient keep. I wait. Soon on the deepened dusk spread his soft wings, out over the meadow he sails, up over my wooded height, over my moat, to my turret tall, as silent and unseen as the soul of a shadow, except he drift across the face of the full round moon, or with his weird cry cause the dreaming quiet to stir in its sleep and moan.

Now let us go over again to the old tree, this time in May. It will be curious enough, as the soft dusk comes on, to see the round face of the owl in one hole and, out of another hole in the broken limb above, the flat, wizened face of a little tree-toad.

Both creatures love the dusk; both have come forth to their open doors to watch the darkening; both will make off under the cover of the night — one for mice and frogs over the meadow, the other for slugs and insects over the crooked, tangled limbs of the apple tree.

It is strange enough to see them together, but it is stranger still to think of them together; for it is just such prey as this little toad that the owl has gone over the meadow to catch.

Why does he not take the supper ready here on the shelf? There may be reasons that we, who do not eat tree-toad, know nothing of; but I am inclined to believe that the owl has never seen his fellow lodger in the doorway above, though he must often have heard him trilling gently and lonesomely in the gloaming, when his skin cries for rain!

Small wonder if they have never met! for this gray, squat, disk-toed little monster in the hole, or flattened on the bark of the tree like a patch of lichen, may well be one of the things that are hidden from even the sharp-eyed owl. It is always a source of fresh amazement, the way that this largest of the hylas, on the moss-marked rind of an old tree, can utterly blot himself out before your staring eyes.

SPRING

The common toads and all the frogs have enemies enough, and it would seem from the comparative scarcity of the tree-toads that they must have enemies, too; but I do not know who they are. This scarcity of the tree-toads is something of a puzzle, and all the more to me, that, to my certain knowledge, this toad has lived in the old Baldwin tree, now, for five years. Perhaps he has been several toads, you say, not one; for who can tell one tree-toad from another? Nobody; and for that reason I made, some time ago, a simple experiment, in order to see how long a tree-toad might live, unprotected, in his own natural environment.

Upon moving into this house, about nine years ago, we found a tree-toad living in the big hickory by the porch. For the next three springs he reappeared, and all summer long we would find him, now on the tree, now on the porch, often on the railing and backed tight up against a post. Was he one or many? we asked. Then we marked him; and for the next four years we knew that he was himself alone. How many more years he might have lived in the hickory for us all to pet, I should like to know; but last summer, to our great sorrow, the gypsy moth killers, poking in the hole, hit our little friend and left him dead.

It was very wonderful to me, the instinct for home — the love for home, I should like to call it — that this humble little creature showed. Now, a toad is an amphibian to the zoologist; an ugly gnome with a jeweled eye, to the poet; but to the naturalist, the lover of life for its own sake, who lives next door to his toad, who feeds him a fly or a fat grub now and then, who tickles him to sleep with a rose leaf, who waits as thirstily as the hilltop for him to call the summer rain, who knows his going to sleep for the winter, his waking up for the spring — to such a one, I say, a tree-toad means more than the jeweled eye and the strange amphibious habits.

This small tree-toad had a home, had it in a tree, too, — in a hickory tree, — this toad that dwelt by my house.

SPRING

"East, west,
Hame 's best,"

croaked our tree-toad in a tremulous, plaintive song that
wakened memories in the vague twilight of more old, unhappy,
far-off things than any other voice I ever knew.

These two tree-toads could not have been induced to trade
houses, the hickory for the apple, because a house to a toad
means home, and a home is never in the market. There are
many more houses in the land than homes. Most of us are
only real-estate dealers. Many of us have never had a home;
and none of us has ever had, perhaps, more than one, or could
have — that home of our childhood.

This toad seemed to feel it all. Here in the hickory for four
years (more nearly seven, I am sure) he lived, single and alone.
He would go down to the meadow when the toads gathered
there to lay their eggs; but back he would come, without mate
or companion, to his tree. Stronger than love of kind, than
love of mate, constant and dominant in his slow cold heart was
his instinct for home.

If I go down to the orchard and bring up from an apple tree
some other toad to dwell in the hole of the hickory, I shall fail.
He might remain for the day, but not throughout the night, for
with the gathering twilight there steals upon him an irresistible
longing; and guided by it, as bee and pigeon and dog and man
are guided, he makes his sure way back to his orchard home.

Would my toad of the Baldwin tree go back beyond the
orchard, over the road, over the wide meadow, over to the old
tree, half a mile away, if I brought him from there? We shall see.
During the coming summer I shall mark him in some manner,
and bringing him here to the hickory, I shall then watch the old
apple tree yonder to see if he returns. It will be a hard, perilous
journey. But his longing will not let him rest; and, guided by his
mysterious sense of direction, for that *one* place, he will arrive,
I am sure, or he will die on the way.

Suppose he never gets back? Only one toad less? A great

deal more than that. There in the old Baldwin he has made his home for I don't know how long, hunting over its world of branches in the summer, sleeping down in its deep holes during the winter — down under the chips and punk and castings, beneath the nest of the owls, it may be; for my toad in the hickory always buried himself so, down in the debris at the bottom of the hole, where, in a kind of cold storage, he preserved himself until thawed out by the spring.

I never pass the old apple in the summer but that I stop to pay my respects to the toad; nor in the winter that I do not pause and think of him asleep in there. He is no longer mere toad. He has passed into the Guardian Spirit of the tree, warring in the green leaf against worm and grub and slug, and in the dry leaf hiding himself, a heart of life, within the thin ribs, as if to save the old shell of a tree to another summer.

Often in the dusk, especially the summer dusk, I have gone over to sit at his feet and learn some of the things that my school-teachers and college professors did not teach me. Seating myself comfortably at the foot of the tree, I wait. The toad comes forth to the edge of his hole above me, settles himself comfortably, and waits. And the lesson begins. The quiet of the summer evening steals out with the wood-shadows and softly covers the fields. We do not stir. An hour passes. We do not stir. Not to stir is the lesson — one of the primary lessons in this course with the toad.

The dusk thickens. The grasshoppers begin to strum; the owl slips out and drifts away; a whippoorwill drops on the bare knoll near me, clucks and shouts and shouts again, his rapid repetition a thousand times repeated by the voices that call to one another down the long empty aisles of the swamp; a big moth whirs about my head and is gone; a bat flits squeaking past; a firefly blazes, is blotted out by the darkness, blazes again, and so passes, his tiny lantern flashing into a night that seems the darker for his quick, unsteady glow.

We do not stir. It is a hard lesson. By all my other teachers I had been taught every manner of stirring, and this strange exercise of being still takes me where my body is weakest, and puts me almost out of breath.

What! out of breath by keeping still? Yes, because I had been hurrying hither and thither, doing this and that — doing them so fast for so many years that I no longer understood how to sit down and keep still and do nothing inside of me as well as outside. Of course *you* know how to keep still, for you are children. And so perhaps you do not need to take lessons of teacher Toad. But I do, for I am grown up, and a man, with a world of things to do, a great many of which I do not need to do at all — if only I would let the toad teach me all he knows.

So, when I am tired, I will go over to the toad. I will sit at his feet, where time is nothing, and the worry of work even less. He has all time and no task. He sits out the hour silent, thinking — I know not what, nor need to know. So we will sit in silence, the toad and I, watching Altair burn along the shore of the horizon, and overhead Arcturus,[1] and the rival fireflies flickering through the leaves of the apple tree. And as we watch, I shall have time to rest and to think. Perhaps I shall have a thought, a thought all my own, a rare thing for any one to have, and worth many an hour of waiting.

---

[1] Altair is the brightest star in the constellation Aquila, the eagle. Arcturus is the brightest star in the constellation Boötes, the herdsman.

IF YOU HAD WINGS

If you had wings, why of course you would wear feathers instead of clothes, and you might be a crow! And then of course you would steal corn, and run the risk of getting three of your big wing feathers shot away.

All winter long, and occasionally during this spring, I have seen one of my little band of crows flying about with a big hole in his wing, — at least three of his large wing feathers gone, shot away probably last summer, — which causes him to fly with a list or limp, like an automobile with a flattened tire, or a ship with a shifted ballast.

Now for nearly a year that crow has been hobbling about on one whole and one half wing, trusting to luck to escape his enemies, until he can get three new feathers to take the places of those that are missing. "Well, why doesn't he get them?" you ask. If you were that crow, how would you get them? Can a crow, by taking thought, add three new feathers to his wing?

Certainly not. That crow must wait until wing-feather season comes again, just as an apple tree must wait until apple-growing season comes to hang its boughs with luscious fruit. The crow has nothing to do with it. His wing feathers are supplied by Nature once a year (after the nesting-time), and if a crow loses any of them, even if right after the new feathers had been supplied, that crow will have to wait until the season for wing feathers comes around once more — if indeed he can wait and does not fall a prey to hawk or owl or the heavy odds of winter.

But Nature is not going to be hurried on that account, nor caused to change one jot or tittle from her wise and methodical course. The Bible says that the hairs of our heads are numbered. So are the feathers on a crow's body. Nature knows just how many there are altogether; how many there are of each sort — primaries, secondaries, tertials, greater coverts, middle coverts, lesser coverts, and scapulars — in the wing; just how each sort

21

is arranged; just when each sort is to be moulted and renewed. If Master Crow does not take care of his clothes, then he will have to go without until the time for a new suit comes; for Mother Nature won't patch them up as your mother patches up yours.

But now this is what I want you to notice and think about: that just as an apple falls according to a great law of Nature, so a bird's feathers fall according to a law of Nature. The moon is appointed for seasons; the sun knoweth his going down; and so light and insignificant a thing as a bird's feather not only is appointed to grow in a certain place at a certain time, but also knoweth its falling off.

Nothing could look more haphazard, certainly, than the way a hen's feathers seem to drop off at moulting time. The most forlorn, undone, abject creature about the farm is the half-moulted hen. There is one in the chicken-yard now, so nearly naked that she really is ashamed of herself, and so miserably helpless that she squats in a corner all night, unable to reach the low poles of the roost. It is a critical experience with the hen, this moulting of her feathers; and were it not for the protection of the yard it would be a fatal experience, so easily could she be captured. Nature seems to have no hand in the business at all; if she has, then what a mess she is making of it!

But pick up the hen, study the falling of the feathers carefully, and lo! here is law and order, every feather as important to Nature as a star, every quill as a planet, and the old white hen as mightily looked after by Nature as the round sphere of the universe!

Once a year, usually after the nesting-season, it seems a physical necessity for most birds to renew their plumage.

We get a new suit (some of us) because our old one wears out. That is the most apparent cause for the new annual suit of the birds. Yet with them, as with some of us, the feathers go out of fashion, and then the change of feathers is a mere matter of style, it seems.

SPRING

For severe and methodical as Mother Nature must be (and what mother or teacher or ruler, who has great things to do and a multitude of little things to attend to, must not be severe and methodical?) — severe, I say, as Mother Nature must be in looking after her children's clothes, she has for all that a real motherly heart, it seems.

For see how she looks after their wedding garments — giving to most of the birds a new suit, gay and gorgeous, especially to the bridegrooms, as if fine feathers *did* make a fine bird! Or does she do all of this to meet the fancy of the bride, as the scientists tell us? Whether so or not, it is a fact that among the birds it is the bridegroom who is adorned for his wife, and sometimes the fine feathers come by a special moult — an extra suit for him!

Take Bobolink, for instance. He has two complete moults a year, two new suits, one of them his wedding suit. Now, as I write, I hear him singing over the meadow — a jet-black, white, and cream-buff lover, most strikingly adorned. His wife, down in the grass, looks as little like him as a sparrow looks like a blackbird. But after the breeding-season he will moult again, changing color so completely that he and his wife and children will all look alike, all like sparrows, and will even lose their names, flying south now under the name of "reedbirds."

Bobolink passes the winter in Brazil; and in the spring, just before the long northward journey begins, he lays aside his fall traveling clothes and puts on his gay wedding garments and starts north for his bride. But you would hardly know he was so dressed, to look at him; for, strangely enough, he is not black and white, but still colored like a sparrow, as he was in the fall. *Apparently* he is. Look at him more closely, however, and you will find that the brownish-yellow color is all caused by a veil of fine fringes hanging from the edges of the feathers. The bridegroom wearing the wedding veil? Yes! Underneath is the black and white and cream-buff suit. He starts northward; and, by the time he reaches Massachusetts, the fringe veil is worn off and the black and white bobolink appears. Specimens taken after their arrival here still show traces of the brownish-yellow veil.

Many birds do not have this early spring moult at all; and with most of those that do, the great wing feathers are not then renewed as are bobolink's, but only at the annual moult after the nesting is done. The great feathers of the wings are, as you know, the most important feathers a bird has; and the shedding of them is so serious a matter that Nature has come to make the change according to the habits and needs of the birds. With most birds the body feathers begin to go first, then the wing feathers, and last those of the tail. But the shedding of the wing feathers is a very slow and carefully regulated process.

In the wild geese and other water birds the wing feathers drop out with the feathers of the body, and go so nearly together that the birds really cannot fly. On land you could catch the birds with your hands. But they keep near or on the water and thus escape, though times have been when it was necessary to protect them at this season by special laws; for bands of men would go into their nesting-marshes and kill them with clubs by hundreds!

The shedding of the feathers brings many risks to the birds; but Nature leaves none of her children utterly helpless. The geese at this time cannot fly because their feathers are gone; but they can swim, and so get away from most of their natural enemies. On the other hand, the hawks that hunt by wing, and must have wings always in good feather, or else perish, lose their feathers so slowly that they never feel their loss. It takes a hawk nearly a year to get a complete change of wing feathers, one or two dropping out from each wing at a time, at long intervals apart.

Then here is the gosling, that goes six weeks in down, before it gets its first feathers, which it sheds within a few weeks, in the fall. Whereas the young quail is born with quills so far grown that it is able to fly almost as soon as it is hatched. These are real mature feathers; but the bird is young and soon

24

outgrows these first flight feathers, so they are quickly lost and new ones come. This goes on till fall, *several* moults occurring the first summer to meet the increasing weight of the little quail's growing body.

I said that Nature was severe and methodical, and she is, where she needs to be, so severe that you are glad, perhaps, that you are not a crow. But Nature, like every wise mother, is severe only where she needs to be. A crow's wing feathers are vastly important to him. Let him then take care of them, for they are the best feathers made and are put in to stay a year. But a crow's tail feathers are not so vastly important to him; he could get on, if, like the rabbit in the old song, he had no tail at all.

In most birds the tail is a kind of balance or steering-gear, and not of equal importance with the wings. Nature, consequently, seems to have attached less importance to the feathers of the tail. They are not so firmly set, nor are they of the same quality or kind; for, unlike the wing feathers, if a tail feather is lost through accident, it is made good, no matter when. How do you explain that? Do you think I believe that old story of the birds roosting with their tails out, so that, because of generations of lost tails, those feathers now grow expecting to be plucked by some enemy, and therefore have only a temporary hold?

The normal, natural way, of course, is to replace a lost feather with a new one as soon as possible. But, in order to give extra strength to the wing feathers, Nature has found it necessary to check their frequent change; and so complete is the check that the annual moult is required to replace a single one. The Japanese have discovered the secret of this check, and are able by it to keep certain feathers in the tails of their cocks growing until they reach the enormous length of ten to twelve feet.

My crow, it seems, lost his three feathers last summer just after his annual moult; the three broken shafts he carries still in his wing, and must continue to carry, as the stars must continue their courses, until those three feathers have rounded out their cycle to the annual moult. The universe of stars and feathers is a universe of law, of order, and of reason.

THE PALACE IN THE PIG-PEN

"You have taken a handful of my wooded acres," says Nature to me, "and if you have not improved them, you at least have changed them greatly. But they are mine still. Be friendly now, go softly, and you shall have them all — and I shall have them all, too. We will share them together."

And we do. Every part of the fourteen acres is mine, yielding some kind of food or fuel or shelter. And every foot, yes, every foot, is Nature's; as entirely hers as when the thick primeval forest stood here. The apple trees are hers as much as mine, and she has ten different bird families that I know of, living in them this spring. A pair of crows and a pair of red-tailed hawks are nesting in the wood-lot; there are at least three families of chipmunks in as many of my stone-piles; a fine old tree-toad sleeps on the porch under the climbing rose; a hornet's nest hangs in a corner of the eaves; a small colony of swifts thunder in the chimney; swallows twitter in the hayloft; a chipmunk and a half-tame gray squirrel feed in the barn; and — to bring an end to this bare beginning — under the roof of the pig-pen dwell a pair of phoebes.

To make a bird-house of a pig-pen, to divide it between the pig and the bird — this is as far as Nature can go, and this is certainly enough to redeem the whole farm. For she has not sent an outcast or a scavenger to dwell in the pen, but a bird of character, however much he may lack in song or color. Phoebe does not make up well in a picture; neither does he perform well as a singer; there is little to him, in fact, but personality — personality of a kind and (may I say?) quantity, sufficient to make the pig-pen a decent and respectable neighborhood.

Phoebe is altogether more than his surroundings. Every time I go to feed the pig, he lights upon a post nearby and says to me, "It's what you are! Not what you do, but how you do it!" — with a launch into the air, a whirl, an unerring snap at a cabbage butterfly, and an easy drop to the post again, by way of illustration. "Not where you live, but how you live there; not

27

the feathers you wear, but how you wear them — it is what you are that counts!"

There is a difference between being a "character" and having one. My Phoebe "lives over the pig," but I cannot feel familiar with a bird of his air and carriage, who faces the world so squarely, who settles upon a stake as if he owned it, who lives a prince in my pig-pen.

Look at him! How alert, able, free! Notice the limber drop of his tail, the ready energy it suggests. By that one sign you would know the bird had force. He is afraid of nothing, not even the cold; and he migrates only because he is a fly-catcher, and is thus compelled to. The earliest spring day, however, that you find the flies buzzing in the sun, look for phoebe. He is back, coming alone and long before it is safe. He was one of the first of my birds to return this spring.

And it was a fearful spring, this of which I am telling you. How Phoebe managed to exist those miserable March days is a mystery. He came directly to the pen as he had come the year before, and his presence in that bleakest of Marches gave the weather its only touch of spring.

The same force and promptness are manifest in the domestic affairs of the bird. One of the first to arrive this spring, he was the first to build and bring off a brood — or, perhaps, *she* was. And the size of the brood — of the broods, for there was a second, and a third!

Phoebe appeared without his mate, and for nearly three weeks he hunted in the vicinity of the pen, calling the day long, and, toward the end of the second week, occasionally soaring into the air, fluttering, and pouring forth a small, ecstatic song that seemed fairly forced from him.

These aerial bursts meant just one thing: *she* was coming, was coming soon! Was she coming or was he getting ready to go for her? Here he had been for nearly three weeks, his house-lot chosen, his mind at rest, his heart beating faster with every sunrise. It was as plain as day that he knew — was certain — just how and just when something lovely was going to happen.

28

I wished I knew. I was half in love with her myself; and I, too, watched for her.

On the evening of April 14th, he was alone as usual. The next morning a pair of phoebes flitted in and out of the windows of the pen. Here she was. Will someone tell me all about it? Had she just come along and fallen instantly in love with him and his fine pig-pen? It is pretty evident that he nested here last year. Was she, then, his old mate? Did they keep together all through the autumn and winter? If so, then why not together all the way back from Florida to Massachusetts?

Here is a pretty story. But who will tell it to me?

For several days after she came, the weather continued raw and wet, so that nest-building was greatly delayed. The scar of an old, last year's nest still showed on a stringer, and I wondered if they had decided on this or some other site for the new nest. They had not made up their minds, for when they did start it was to make three beginnings in as many places.

Then I offered a suggestion. Out of a bit of stick, branching at right angles, I made a little bracket and tacked it up on one of the stringers. It appealed to them at once, and from that moment the building went steadily on.

Saddled upon this bracket, and well mortared to the stringer, the nest, when finished, was as safe as a castle. And how perfect a thing it was! Few nests, indeed, combine the solidity, the softness, and the exquisite inside curve of Phoebe's.

In placing the bracket, I had carelessly nailed it under one of the cracks in the loose board roof. The nest was receiving its first linings when there came a long, hard rain that beat through the crack and soaked the little cradle. This was serious, for a great deal of mud had been worked into the thick foundation, and here, in the constant shade, the dampness would be long in drying out.

The builders saw the mistake, too, and with their great good sense immediately began to remedy it. They built the bottom up thicker, carried the walls over on a slant that brought the outermost point within the line of the crack, then raised them

29

until the cup was as round-rimmed and hollow as the mould of Mrs. Phoebe's breast could make it.

The outside of the nest, its base, is broad and rough and shapeless enough; but nothing could be softer and lovelier than the inside, the cradle, and nothing drier, for the slanting walls of the nest shed every drop from the leafy crack above.

Wet weather followed the heavy rain until long after the nest was finished. The whole structure was as damp and cold as a newly plastered house. It felt wet to my touch. Yet I noticed that the birds were already brooding. Every night and often during the day I would see one of them in the nest — so deep in, that only a head or a tail showed over the round rim.

After several days I looked to see the eggs, but to my surprise found the nest empty. It had been robbed, I thought, yet by what creature I could not imagine. Then down cuddled one of the birds again, and I understood. Instead of wet and cold, the nest to-day was warm to my hand, and dry almost to the bottom. It had changed color, too, all the upper part having turned a soft silver-gray. She (I am sure it was she) had not been brooding her eggs at all; she had been brooding her mother's thought of them; and for them had been nestling here these days and nights, *drying and warming* their damp cradle with the fire of her life and love.

In due time the eggs came, five of them, white, spotless, and shapely. While the little phoebe hen was hatching them, I gave my attention further to the cock.

Our intimate friendship revealed a most pleasing nature in Phoebe. Perhaps such close and continued association would show like qualities in every bird, even in the kingbird; but I fear only a woman, like Mrs. Olive Thorne Miller,[2] could find them in him. Not much can be said of this flycatcher family, except that it is useful — a kind of virtue that gets its chief

---

[2] Harriet Mann Miller (1831–1918) was a naturalist, ornithologist and children's writer who sometimes wrote under the pseudonym Olive Thorne Miller.

reward in heaven. I am acquainted with only four of the other nine Eastern members, — crested flycatcher, kingbird, wood pewee, and chebec, — and each of these has some redeeming attribute besides the habit of catching flies.

They are all good nest-builders, good parents, and brave, independent birds; but aside from phoebe and pewee — the latter in his small way the sweetest voice of the oak woods — the whole family is an odd lot, cross-grained, cross-looking, and about as musical as a family of ducks. A duck seems to know that he cannot sing. A flycatcher knows nothing of his shortcomings. He believes he can sing, and in time he will prove it. If desire and effort count for anything, he certainly must prove it in time. How long the family has already been training, no one knows. Everybody knows, however, the success each flycatcher of them has thus far attained. It would make a good minstrel show, doubtless, if the family would appear together. In chorus, surely, they would be far from a tuneful choir. Yet individually, in the wide universal chorus of the out-of-doors, how much we should miss the kingbird's metallic twitter and the chebec's insistent call!

There was little excitement for phoebe during this period of incubation. He hunted in the neighborhood and occasionally called to his mate, contented enough but certainly sometimes appearing tired.

One rainy day he sat in the pig-pen window looking out at the gray, wet world. He was humped and silent and meditative, his whole attitude speaking the extreme length of his day, the monotony of the drip, drip, drip from the eaves, and the sitting, the ceaseless sitting, of his brooding wife. He might have hastened the time by catching a few flies for her or by taking her place on the nest; but I never saw him do it.

Things were livelier when the eggs hatched, for it required a good many flies a day to keep the five young ones growing. And how they grew! Like bread sponge in a pan, they began to rise, pushing the mother up so that she was forced to stand over them; then pushing her out until she could cling only to the side of the nest at night; then pushing her off altogether. By this time they were hanging to the outside themselves, covering the nest from sight almost, until finally they spilled off upon their wings.

Out of the nest upon the air! Out of the pen and into a sweet, wide world of green and blue and of golden light! I saw one of the broods take this first flight, and it was thrilling.

The nest was placed back from the window and below it, so that in leaving the nest the young would have to drop, then turn and fly up to get out. Below was the pig.

As they grew, I began to fear that they might try their wings before this feat could be accomplished, and so fall to the pig below. But Nature, in this case, was careful of her pearls. Day after day they clung to the nest, even after they might have flown; and when they did go, it was with a sure and long flight that carried them out and away to the tops of the neighboring trees.

They left the nest one at a time and were met in the air by their mother, who, darting to them, calling loudly, and, whirling about them, helped them as high and as far away as they could go.

I wish the simple record of these family affairs could be closed without one tragic entry. But that can rarely be of any family. Seven days after the first brood were awing, I found the new eggs in the nest. Soon after that the male bird disappeared.

The second brood had now been out a week, and in all that time no sight or sound was had of the father.

What happened? Was he killed? Caught by a cat or a hawk? It is possible; and this is an easy and kindly way to think of him. It is not impossible that he may have remained as leader and protector to the first brood; or (perish the thought!) might he have grown weary at sight of the second lot of five eggs, of the long days and the neglect that they meant for him, and out of jealousy and fickleness wickedly deserted?

I hope it was death, a stainless, even ignominious death by

one of my neighbor's many cats.

Death or desertion, it involved a second tragedy. Five such young ones at this time were too many for the mother. She fought nobly; no mother could have done more. All five were brought within a few days of flight; then, one day, I saw a little wing hanging listlessly over the side of the nest. I went closer. One had died. It had starved to death. There were none of the parasites in the nest that often kill whole broods. It was a plain case of sacrifice, — by the mother, perhaps; by the other young, maybe — one for the other four.

But she did well. Nine such young birds to her credit since April. Who shall measure her actual use to the world? How does she compare in value with the pig? Weeks later I saw several of her brood along the meadow fence hawking for flies. They were not far from my cabbage-patch.

I hope a pair of them will return to me next spring and that they will come early. Any bird that deigns to dwell under roof of mine commands my friendship. But no other bird takes Phoebe's place in my affections; there is so much in him to like, and he speaks for so much of the friendship of nature.

"Humble and inoffensive bird" he has been called by one of our leading ornithologies — because he comes to my pig-pen! Inoffensive! this bird with the cabbage butterfly in his beak! The faint and damning praise! And humble? There is not a humble feather on his body. Humble to those who see the pen and not the bird. But to me — why, the bird has made a palace of my pig-pen!

The very pig seems less a pig because of this exquisite association; and the lowly work of feeding the creature has been turned for me by Phoebe into a poetic course in bird study.

THE BUZZARD OF THE BEAR SWAMP

No, I do not believe that any one of you ever went into a swamp to find a turkey buzzard's nest. Still, if you had been born on the edge of a great swamp, as I was, and if the great-winged buzzards had been soaring, soaring up in your sky, as all through my boyhood they were soaring up in mine, then why should you not have gone some time into the swamp to see where they make their nests — these strange cloud-winged creatures?

Boys are boys, and girls are girls, the world over; and I am pretty sure that little Jack Horner and myself were not the only two boys in all the world to do great and wonderful deeds. Any boy with a love for birds and a longing for the deep woods, living close to the edge of the Bear Swamp, would have searched out that buzzard's nest.

Although I was born within the shadows of the Bear Swamp, close enough to smell the magnolias along its margin, and lived my first ten years only a little farther off, yet it was not until after twice ten years of absence that I stood again within sight of it, ready for the first time to cross its dark borders and find the buzzard's nest.

Now here at last I found myself, looking down over the largest, least trod, deepest-tangled swamp in southern New Jersey — wide, gloomy, silent, and to me, — for I still thought of it as I used to when a child, — to me, a mysterious realm of black streams, hollow trees, animal trails, and haunting shapes, presided over by this great bird, the turkey buzzard.

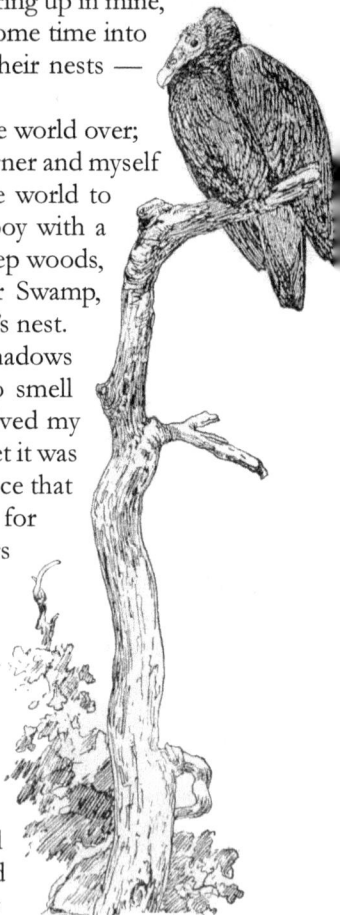

SPRING

For he was never mere bird to me, but some kind of spirit. He stood to me for what was far off, mysterious, secret, and unapproachable in the deep, dark swamp; and, in the sky, so wide were his wings, so majestic the sweep of his flight, he had always stirred me, caused me to hold my breath and wish myself to fly.

No other bird did I so much miss from my New England skies when I came here to live. Only the other day, standing in the heart of Boston, I glanced up and saw, sailing at a far height against the billowy clouds, an aeroplane; and what should I think of but the flight of the vulture, so like the steady wings of the great bird seemed the steady wings of this great monoplane far off against the sky.

And so you begin to understand why I had come back after so many years to the swamp, and why I wanted to see the nest of this strange bird that had been flying, flying forever in my imagination and in my sky. But my good uncle, whom I was visiting, when I mentioned my quest, merely exclaimed, "What in thunderation!"

You will find a good many uncles and other folk who won't understand a good many things that you want to do. Never mind. If you want to see a buzzard's nest, let all your relations exclaim while you go quietly off alone and see it.

I wanted to find a buzzard's nest — the nest of the Bear Swamp buzzard; and here at last I stood; and yonder on the clouds, a mere mote in the distance, floated the bird. It was coming toward me over the wide reach of the swamp.

Silent, inscrutable, and alien lay the swamp, and untouched by human hands. Over it spread a quiet and reserve as real as twilight. Like a mask it was worn, and was slipped on, I know, at my approach. I could feel the silent spirit of the place drawing back away from me. But I should have at least a guide to lead me through the shadow land, for out of the lower living green towered a line of limbless stubs, like a line of telegraph-poles, their bleached bones gleaming white, or showing dark and gaunt against the horizon, and marking for me a path far out across the swamp. Besides, here came the buzzard winding slowly down the clouds. Soon its spiral changed to a long pendulum-swing, till just above the skeleton trees the great bird wheeled and, bracing itself with its flapping wings, dropped heavily upon one of the headless tree-trunks.

It had come leisurely, yet I could see that it had come with a directness and purpose that was unmistakable and also meaningful. It had discovered me in the distance, and, while still invisible to my eyes, had started down to perch upon that giant stub in order to watch me. It was suspicious, and had come to watch me, because somewhere beneath its perch, I felt sure, lay a hollow log, the creature's den, holding its two eggs or its young. A buzzard has something like a soul.

Marking the direction of the stub, and its probable distance, I waded into the deep underbrush, the buzzard perched against the sky for my guide, and, for my quest, the stump or hollow log that held the creature's nest.

The rank ferns and ropy vines swallowed me up, and shut out at times even the sight of the sky and the buzzard. It was not until half an hour's struggle that, climbing a pine-crested swell in the low bottom, I sighted the bird again. It had not moved.

I was now in the real swamp, the old uncut forest. It was a land of tree giants: huge tulip poplar and swamp white oak, so old that they had become solitary, their comrades having fallen one by one; while some of them, unable to loose their grip upon the soil, which had widened and tightened through centuries, were still standing, though long since dead. It was upon one of these that the buzzard sat humped.

Directly in my path stood an ancient swamp white oak, the greatest tree, I think, that I have ever seen. It was not the highest, nor the largest round, perhaps, but in years and looks the greatest. Hoary, hollow, and broken-limbed, his huge bole seemed encircled with the centuries.

SPRING

"For it had bene an auncient tree,
Sacred with many a mysteree."

Above him to twice his height loomed a tulip poplar, clean-boled for thirty feet and in the top all green and gold with blossoms. It was a resplendent thing beside the oak, yet how unmistakably the gnarled old monarch wore the crown! His girth more than balanced the poplar's greater height; and, as for blossoms, he had his tiny-flowered catkins; but nature knows the beauty of strength and inward majesty, and has pinned no boutonnière upon the oak.

My buzzard now was hardly more than half a mile away, and plainly seen through the rifts in the lofty timbered roof above me. As I was nearing the top of a large fallen pine that lay in my course, I was startled by the *burrh! burrh! burrh!* of three partridges taking wing just beyond, near the foot of the tree. Their exploding flight seemed all the more like a real explosion when three little clouds of dust-smoke rose out of the low, *wet* bottom of the swamp and drifted up against the green.

Then I saw an interesting sight. The pine, in its fall, had snatched with its wide-reaching, multitudinous roots at the shallow bottom and torn out a giant fistful of earth, leaving a hole about two feet deep and more than a dozen feet wide. The sand thus lifted into the air had gradually washed down into a mound on each side of the butt, where it lay high and dry above the level of the wet swamp. This the swamp birds had turned into a great dust-bath. It was in constant use, evidently. Not a spear of grass had sprouted in it, and all over it were pits and craters of various sizes, showing that not only the partridges but also the quail and such small things as the warblers bathed here, — though I can't recall ever having seen a warbler bathe in the dust. A dry bath in the swamp was something of a luxury, evidently. I wonder if the buzzards used it?

I went forward cautiously now, and expectantly, for I was close enough to see the white beak and red wattled neck of my buzzard guide. The buzzard saw me, too, and began to twist its head and to twitch its wing-tips nervously. Then the long, black wings began to open, as you would open a two-foot rule, and, with a heavy lurch that left the dead stub rocking, the bird dropped and was soon soaring high up in the blue.

This was the locality of the nest; now where should I find it? Evidently I was to have no further help from the old bird. The underbrush was so thick that I could hardly see farther than my nose. A half-rotten tree-trunk lay near, the top end resting across the backs of several saplings that it had borne down in its fall. I crept up on this for a look around, and almost tumbled off at finding myself staring directly into the dark, cavernous hollow of an immense log lying on a slight rise of ground a few feet ahead of me.

It was a yawning hole, which at a glance I knew belonged to the buzzard. The log, a mere shell of a mighty white oak, had been girdled and felled with an axe, by coon-hunters probably, and still lay with one side resting upon the rim of the stump. As I stood looking, something white stirred vaguely in the hole and disappeared.

Leaping from my perch, I scrambled forward to the mouth of the hollow log and was greeted with hisses from far back in the dark. Then came a thumping of bare feet, more hisses, and a sound of snapping beaks. I had found my buzzard's nest!

Hardly that, either, for there was not a feather, stick, or chip as evidence of a nest. The eggs had been laid upon the sloping cavern floor, and in the course of their incubation must have rolled clear down to the opposite end, where the opening was so narrow that the buzzard could not have brooded them until she had rolled them back. The wonder is that they had ever hatched.

But they had, and what they hatched was another wonder. Nature never intended a young buzzard for any eye but his mother's, and *she* hates the sight of him. Elsewhere I have told of a buzzard that devoured her eggs at the approach of an enemy, so delicately balanced are her unnamable appetites and her maternal affections!

SPRING

The two strange nestlings in the log must have been three weeks old, I should say, the larger weighing about four pounds. They were covered, as young owls are, with deep snow-white down, out of which protruded their black scaly, snaky legs. They stood braced on these long black legs, their receding heads drawn back, shoulders thrust forward, and bodies humped between the featherless wings like challenging tom-cats.

In order to examine them, I crawled into the den — not a difficult act, for the opening measured four feet and a half across at the mouth. The air was musty inside, yet surprisingly free from odor. The floor was absolutely clean, but on the top and sides of the cavity was a thick coating of live mosquitoes, most of them gorged, hanging like a red-beaded tapestry over the walls.

I had taken pains that the flying buzzard should not see me enter, for I hoped she would descend to look after her young. But she would take no chances with herself. I sat near the mouth of the hollow, where I could catch the fresh breeze that pulled across the end, and where I had a view of a far-away bit of sky. Suddenly, across this field of blue, there swept a meteor of black — the buzzard! and evidently in that instant of passage, at a distance certainly of half a mile, she spied me in the log.

I waited more than an hour longer, and when I tumbled out with a dozen kinds of cramps, the unworried mother was soaring serenely far up in the clear, cool sky.

TURTLE EGGS FOR AGASSIZ

I took down, recently, from the shelves of a great public library, the four volumes of Agassiz's *Contributions to the Natural History of the United States*. I doubt if anybody but the charwoman, with her duster, had touched those volumes for twenty-five years. They are a monumental work, the fruit of vast and heroic labors, with colored plates on stone, showing the turtles of the United States, and their life-history. The work was published more than half a century ago, but it looked old beyond its years — massive, heavy, weathered, as if dug from the rocks; and I soon turned with a sigh from the weary learning of its plates and diagrams to look at the preface.[3]

Then, reading down through the catalogue of human names and of thanks for help received, I came to a sentence beginning: —

"In New England I have myself collected largely; but I have also received valuable contributions from the late Rev. Zadoc Thompson of Burlington; . . . from Mr. D. Henry Thoreau of Concord ; . . . and from Mr. J. W. P. Jenks of Middleboro'." And then it hastens on with the thanks in order to get to the turtles, as if turtles were the one and only thing of real importance in all the world.

Turtles are important — interesting; so is the late Rev. Zadoc Thompson of Burlington. Indeed any reverend gentleman who would catch turtles for Agassiz must have been interesting. If Agassiz had only put a chapter into his turtle book about him!

---

[3] Louis Agassiz. *Contributions to the Natural History of the United States of America*. Boston: Little, Brown and Co.; London: Trubner & Co., 1857-1862. Blum describes these four quarto volumes as "perhaps the most elaborately produced American zoological production of mid-century." Two years before Darwin's *On the Origin of Species* (1859), Agassiz argues that close study of natural history conclusively demonstrates a creative thoughtfulness only achievable by a higher being.

and as for the Mr. Jenks of Middleboro' (at the end of the quotation) I know that he was interesting; for years later, he was an old college professor of mine. He told me some of the particulars of his turtle contributions, particulars which Agassiz should have found a place for in his big book. The preface says merely that this gentleman sent turtles to Cambridge by the thousands — brief and scanty recognition. For that is not the only thing this gentleman did. On one occasion he sent, not turtles, but turtle *eggs* to Cambridge — *brought* them, I should say; and all there is to show for it, so far as I could discover, is a small drawing of a bit of one of the eggs!

Of course, Agassiz wanted to make that drawing, and had to have a *fresh* turtle egg to draw it from. He had to have it, and he got it. A great man, when he wants a certain turtle egg, at a certain time, always gets it, for he gets someone else to get it for him. I am glad he got it. But what makes me sad and impatient is that he did not think it worthwhile to tell us about the getting of it.

It would seem, naturally, that there could be nothing unusual or interesting about the getting of turtle eggs when you want them. Nothing at all, if you should chance to want the eggs as you chance to find them. So with anything else. But if you want turtle eggs *when* you want them, and are bound to have them, then you must get Mr. Jenks, or somebody else to get them for you.

Agassiz wanted those turtle eggs when he wanted them — not a minute over three hours from the minute they were laid. Yet even that does not seem exacting, hardly more difficult than the getting of hens' eggs only three hours old. Just so, provided the professor could have had his private turtle-coop in Harvard College Yard; and provided he could have made his turtles lay. But turtles will not respond, like hens, to meat-scraps and the warm mash. The professor's problem was not to get from a mud turtle's nest in the back yard to his work-table in the laboratory; but to get from the laboratory in Cambridge to some pond when the turtles were laying, and back to the laboratory within the limited time. And this might have called for nice and discriminating work — as it did.

Agassiz had been engaged for a long time upon his *Contributions*. He had brought the great work nearly to a finish. It was, indeed, finished but for one small yet very important bit of observation: he had carried the turtle egg through every stage of its development with the single exception of one — the very earliest. That beginning stage had brought the *Contributions* to a halt. To get eggs that were fresh enough to show the incubation at this period had been impossible.

There were several ways that Agassiz might have proceeded: he might have got a leave of absence for the spring term, taken his laboratory to some pond inhabited by turtles, and there camped until he should catch the reptile digging out her nest. But there were difficulties in all of that — as those who are college professors and naturalists know. As this was quite out of the question, he did the easiest thing — asked Mr. Jenks of Middleboro to get him the eggs. Mr. Jenks got them. Agassiz knew all about his getting of them; and I say the strange and irritating thing is, that Agassiz did not think it worthwhile to tell us about it, at least in the preface to his monumental work.

It was many years later that Mr. Jenks, then a gray-haired college professor, told me how he got those eggs to Agassiz.

"I was principal of an academy, during my younger years," he began, "and was busy one day with my classes, when a large man suddenly filled the doorway of the room, smiled to the four corners of the room, and called out with a big, quick voice that he was Professor Agassiz.

"Of course he was. I knew it, even before he had had time to shout it to me across the room.

"Would I get him some turtle eggs? he called. Yes, I would. And would I get them to Cambridge within three hours from the time they were laid? Yes, I would. And I did. And it was worth the doing. But I did it only once.

"When I promised Agassiz those eggs, I knew where I was going to get them. I had got turtle eggs there before — at

42

a particular patch of sandy shore along a pond, a few miles distant from the academy.

"Three hours was the limit. From the railroad station to Boston was thirty-five miles; from the pond to the station was perhaps three or four miles; from Boston to Cambridge we called about three miles. Forty miles in round numbers! We figured it all out before he returned, and got the trip down to two hours, — record time: — driving from the pond to the station; from the station by express train to Boston; from Boston by cab to Cambridge. This left an easy hour for accidents and delays.

"Cab and car and carriage we reckoned into our time-table; but what we didn't figure on was the turtle." And he paused abruptly.

"Young man," he went on, his shaggy brows and spectacles hardly hiding the twinkle in the eyes that were bent severely upon me, "young man, when *you* go after turtle eggs, take into account the turtle. No! No! that's bad advice. Youth never reckons on the turtle — and youth seldom ought to. Only old age does that; and old age would never have got those turtle eggs to Agassiz.

"It was in the early spring that Agassiz came to the academy, long before there was any likelihood of the turtles' laying. But I was eager for the quest, and so fearful of failure that I started out to watch at the pond, fully two weeks ahead of the time that the turtles might be expected to lay. I remember the date clearly: it was May 14th.

"A little before dawn — along near three o'clock — I would drive over to the pond, hitch my horse nearby, settle myself quietly among some thick cedars close to the sandy shore, and there I would wait, my kettle of sand ready, my eye covering the whole sleeping pond. Here among the cedars I would eat my breakfast, and then get back in good season to open the academy for the morning session.

"And so the watch began.

"I soon came to know individually the dozen or more

43

turtles that kept to my side of the pond. Shortly after the cold mist would lift and melt away, they would stick up their heads through the quiet water; and as the sun slanted down over the ragged rim of tree-tops, the slow things would float into the warm lighted spots, or crawl out and doze comfortably on the hummocks and snags.

"What fragrant mornings those were! How fresh and new and unbreathed! The pond odors, the woods odors, the odors of the ploughed fields — of water-lily, and wild grape, and the dew-laid soil! I can taste them yet, and hear them yet — the still, large sounds of the waking day — the pickerel breaking the quiet with his swirl; the kingfisher dropping anchor; the stir of feet and wings among the trees. And then the thought of the great book being held up for me! Those were rare mornings!

"But there began to be a good many of them, for the turtles showed no desire to lay. They sprawled in the sun, and never one came out upon the sand as if she intended to help on the great professor's book. The story of her eggs was of small concern to her; her contribution to the Natural History of the United States could wait.

"And it did wait. I began my watch on the 14th of May; June 1st found me still among the cedars, still waiting, as I had waited every morning, Sundays and rainy days alike. June 1st was a perfect morning, but every turtle slid out upon her log, as if egg-laying might be a matter strictly of next year.

"I began to grow uneasy, — not impatient yet, for a naturalist learns his lesson of patience early, and for all his years; but I began to fear lest, by some subtile sense, my presence might somehow be known to the creatures; that they might have gone to some other place to lay, while I was away at the schoolroom.

"I watched on to the end of the first week, on to the end of the second week in June, seeing the mists rise and vanish every morning, and along with them vanish, more and more, the poetry of my early morning vigil. Poetry and rheumatism cannot long dwell together in the same clump of cedars, and I had begun to feel the rheumatism. A month of morning mists wrapping me around had at last soaked through to my bones. But Agassiz was waiting, and the world was waiting, for those turtle eggs; and I would wait. It was all I could do, for there is no use bringing a china nest-egg to a turtle; she is not open to any such delicate suggestion.

"Then came a mid-June Sunday morning, with dawn breaking a little after three: a warm, wide-awake dawn, with the level mist lifted from the level surface of the pond a full hour higher than I had seen it any morning before.

"This was the day. I knew it. I have heard persons say that they can hear the grass grow; that they know by some extra sense when danger is nigh. For a month I had been watching, had been brooding over this pond, and now I knew. I felt a stirring of the pulse of things that the cold-hearted turtles could no more escape than could the clods and I.

"Leaving my horse unhitched, as if he, too, understood, I slipped eagerly into my covert for a look at the pond. As I did so, a large pickerel ploughed a furrow out through the spatter-docks, and in his wake rose the head of a large painted turtle. Swinging slowly round, the creature headed straight for the shore, and, without a pause, scrambled out on the sand.

"She was nothing unusual for a turtle, but her manner was unusual and the gait at which she moved; for there was method in it and fixed purpose. On she came, shuffling over the sand toward the higher open fields, with a hurried, determined, see-saw that was taking her somewhere in particular, and that was bound to get her there on time.

"I held my breath. Had she been a dinosaurian making Mesozoic footprints, I could not have been more fearful. For footprints in the Mesozoic mud, or in the sands of time, were as nothing to me when compared with fresh turtle eggs in the sands of this pond.

"But over the strip of sand, without a stop, she paddled, and up a narrow cow-path into the high grass along a fence. Then up the narrow cow-path, on all fours, just like another turtle, I paddled, and into the high wet grass along the fence.

"I kept well within sound of her, for she moved recklessly, leaving a wide trail of flattened grass behind. I wanted to stand up, — and I don't believe I could have turned her back with a rail, — but I was afraid if she saw me that she might return indefinitely to the pond; so on I went, flat to the ground, squeezing through the lower rails of the fence, as if the field beyond were a melon-patch. It was nothing of the kind, only a wild, uncomfortable pasture, full of dewberry vines, and very discouraging. They were excessively wet vines and briery. I pulled my coat-sleeves as far over my fists as I could get them, and with the tin pail of sand swinging from between my teeth to avoid noise, I stumped fiercely, but silently, on after the turtle.

"She was laying her course, I thought, straight down the length of this dreadful pasture, when, not far from the fence, she suddenly hove to, warped herself short about, and came back, barely clearing me. I warped about, too, and in her wake bore down across the corner of the pasture, across the powdery public road, and on to a fence along a field of young corn.

"I was somewhat wet by this time, but not so wet as I had been before wallowing through the deep, dry dust of the road. Hurrying up behind a large tree by the fence, I peered down the corn-rows and saw the turtle stop, and begin to paw about in the loose, soft soil. She was going to lay!

"I held on to the tree and watched, as she tried this place, and that place, and the other place. But *the* place, evidently, was hard to find. What could a female turtle do with a whole field of possible nests to choose from? Then at last she found it, and, whirling about, she backed quickly at it and, tail first, began to bury herself before my staring eyes.

"Those were not the supreme moments of my life; perhaps those moments came later that day; but those certainly were among the slowest, most dreadfully mixed of moments that I ever experienced. They were hours long. There she was, her

46

shell just showing, like some old hulk in the sand alongshore. And how long would she stay there? and how should I know if she had laid an egg?

"I could still wait. And so I waited, when, over the freshly awakened fields, floated four mellow strokes from the distant town clock.

"Four o'clock! Why there was no train until seven! No train for three hours! The eggs would spoil! Then with a rush it came over me that this was Sunday morning, and there was no regular seven o'clock train, — none till after nine.

"I think I should have fainted had not the turtle just then begun crawling off. I was weak and dizzy; but there, there in the sand, were the eggs! And Agassiz! and the great book! Why, I cleared the fence — and the forty miles that lay between me and Cambridge — at a single jump! He should have them, trains or no. Those eggs should go to Agassiz by seven o'clock, if I had to gallop every mile of the way. Forty miles! Any horse could cover it in three hours, if he had to; and, upsetting the astonished turtle, I scooped out her long white eggs.

"On a bed of sand in the bottom of the pail I laid them, with what care my trembling fingers allowed; filled in between them with more sand; so with layer after layer to the rim; and covering all smoothly with more sand, I ran back for my horse.

"That horse knew, as well as I, that the turtles had laid, and that he was to get those eggs to Agassiz. He turned out of that field into the road on two wheels, a thing he had not done for twenty years, doubling me up before the dashboard, the pail of eggs miraculously lodged between my knees.

"I let him out. If only he could keep this pace all the way to Cambridge! — or even halfway there, I would have time to finish the trip on foot. I shouted him on, holding to the dasher with one hand, holding the pail of eggs with the other, not daring to get off my knees, though the bang on them, as we pounded down the wood-road, was terrific. But nothing must happen to the eggs; they must not be jarred, or even turned over in the sand before they came to Agassiz.

"In order to get out on the pike it was necessary to drive back away from Boston toward the town. We had nearly covered the distance, and were rounding a turn from the woods into the open fields, when, ahead of me, at the station it seemed, I heard the quick, sharp whistle of a locomotive.

"What did it mean? Then followed the *puff, puff, puff,* of a starting train. But what train? Which way going? And jumping to my feet for a longer view, I pulled into a side road that paralleled the track, and headed hard for the station.

"We reeled along. The station was still out of sight, but from behind the bushes that shut it from view, rose the smoke of a moving engine. It was perhaps a mile away, but we were approaching, head on, and, topping a little hill, I swept down upon a freight train, the black smoke pouring from the stack, as the mighty creature pulled itself together for its swift run down the rails.

"My horse was on the gallop, following the track, and going straight toward the coming train. The sight of it almost maddened me — the bare thought of it, on the road to Boston! On I went; on it came, a half a quarter of a mile between us, when suddenly my road shot out along an unfenced field with only a level stretch of sod between me and the engine.

"With a pull that lifted the horse from his feet, I swung him into the field and sent him straight as an arrow for the track. That train should carry me and my eggs to Boston !

"The engineer pulled the whistle. He saw me stand up in the rig, saw my hat blow off, saw me wave my arms, saw the tin pail swing in my teeth, and he jerked out a succession of sharp Halts! But it was he who should halt, not I; and on we went, the horse with a flounder landing the carriage on top of the track.

"The train was already grinding to a stop; but before it was near a standstill, I had backed off the track, jumped out, and, running down the rails with the astonished engineers gaping at me, had swung aboard the cab.

"They offered no resistance; they hadn't had time. Nor did they have the disposition, for I looked strange, not to say dangerous. Hatless, dew-soaked, smeared with yellow mud, and holding, as if it were a baby or a bomb, a little tin pail of sand!

"'Crazy,' the fireman muttered, looking to the engineer for his cue.

"I had been crazy, perhaps, but I was not crazy now.

"'Throw her wide open,' I commanded. 'Wide open! These are fresh turtle eggs for Professor Agassiz of Cambridge. He must have them before breakfast.'

"Then they knew I was crazy, and, evidently thinking it best to humor me, threw the throttle wide open, and away we went.

"I kissed my hand to the horse, grazing unconcernedly in the open field, and gave a smile to my crew. That was all I could give them, and hold myself and the eggs together. But the smile was enough. And they smiled through their smut at me, though one of them held fast to his shovel, while the other kept his hand upon a big ugly wrench. Neither of them spoke to me, but above the roar of the swaying engine I caught enough of their broken talk to understand that they were driving under a full head of steam, with the intention of handing me over to the Boston police, as perhaps the safest way of disposing of me.

"I was only afraid that they would try it at the next station. But that station whizzed past without a bit of slack, and the next, and the next; when it came over me that this was the through freight, which should have passed in the night, and was making up lost time.

"Only the fear of the shovel and the wrench kept me from shaking hands with both men at this discovery. But I beamed at them; and they at me. I was enjoying it. The unwonted jar beneath my feet was wrinkling my diaphragm with spasms of delight. And the fireman beamed at the engineer, with a look that said, 'See the lunatic grin; he likes it!'

"He did like it. How the iron wheels sang to me as they took the rails! How the rushing wind in my ears sang to me! From my stand on the fireman's side of the cab I could catch a glimpse of the track just ahead of the engine, where the ties seemed to leap into the throat of the mile-devouring monster. The joy of it! of seeing space swallowed by the mile!

"I shifted the eggs from hand to hand and thought of my horse, of Agassiz, of the great book, of my great luck, — luck, — luck, — until the multitudinous tongues of the thundering train were all chiming 'luck! luck! luck!' They knew! they understood! This beast of fire and tireless wheels was doing its best to get the eggs to Agassiz!

"We swung out past the Blue Hills, and yonder flashed the morning sun from the towering dome of the State House. I might have leaped from the cab and run the rest of the way on foot, had I not caught the eye of the engineer watching me narrowly. I was not in Boston yet, nor in Cambridge either. I was an escaped lunatic, who had held up a train, and forced it to carry me from Middleboro to Boston.

"Perhaps I had overdone the lunacy business. Suppose these two men should take it into their heads to turn me over to the police, whether I would or no? I could never explain the case in time to get the eggs to Agassiz. I looked at my watch. There were still a few minutes left in which I might explain to these men, who, all at once, had become my captors. But how explain? Nothing could avail against my actions, my appearance, and my little pail of sand.

"I had not thought of my appearance before. Here I was, face and clothes caked with yellow mud, my hair wild and matted, my hat gone, and in my full-grown hands a tiny tin pail of sand, as if I had been digging all night with a tiny tin shovel on the shore! And thus to appear in the decent streets of Boston of a Sunday morning!

"I began to *feel* like a lunatic. The situation was serious, or might be, and rather desperately funny at its best. I must in some way have shown my new fears, for both men watched me more sharply.

"Suddenly, as we were nearing the outer freight-yard, the train slowed down and came to a stop. I was ready to jump, but still I had no chance. They had nothing to do, apparently, but to guard me. I looked at my watch again. What time we had made! It was only six o'clock, a whole hour left in which to get to Cambridge!

"But I didn't like this delay. Five minutes — ten — went by.

"'Gentlemen,' I began, but was cut short by an express train coming past. We were moving again, on — into a siding — on to the main track — on with a bump and a crash and a succession of crashes, running the length of the train — on, on at a turtle's pace, but on, — when the fireman, quickly jumping for the bell-rope, left the way to the step free, and —

"I never touched the step, but landed in the soft sand at the side of the track, and made a line for the freight-yard fence.

"There was no hue or cry. I glanced over my shoulder to see if they were after me. Evidently their hands were full, or they didn't know I had gone.

"But I had gone; and was ready to drop over the high board-fence, when it occurred to me that I might drop into a policeman's arms. Hanging my pail in a splint on top of a post, I peered cautiously over — a very wise thing to do before you jump a high board-fence. There, crossing the open square toward the station, was a big, burly fellow with a club looking for me!

"I flattened for a moment, when someone in the freight-yard yelled at me. I preferred the policeman, and, grabbing my pail, I slid softly over to the street. The policeman moved on past the corner of the station out of sight. The square was free, and yonder stood a cab.

"Time was flying now. Here was the last lap. The cabman saw me coming, and squared away. I waved a dollar-bill at him, but he only stared the more. A dollar can cover a good deal, but I was too much for one dollar. I pulled out another, thrust them both at him, and dodged into the cab, calling, "Cambridge!"

"He would have taken me straight to the police-station, had I not said, 'Harvard College. Professor Agassiz's house! I've got eggs for Agassiz,' pushing another dollar up at him through the hole.

"It was nearly half past six.

"'Let him go!' I ordered. 'Here's another dollar if you make Agassiz's house in twenty minutes. Let him out; never mind the police!'

"He evidently knew the police, or there were none around at that time on a Sunday morning. We went down the sleeping streets, as I had gone down the wood-roads from the pond two hours before, but with the rattle and crash now of a fire brigade. Whirling a corner into Cambridge Street, we took the bridge at a gallop, the driver shouting out something in Hibernian to a pair of waving arms and a belt and brass buttons.

"Across the bridge with a rattle and jolt that put the eggs in jeopardy, and on over the cobble-stones, we went. Half standing, to lessen the jar, I held the pail in one hand and held myself in the other, not daring to let go even to look at my watch.

"But I was afraid to look at the watch. I was afraid to see how near to seven o'clock it might be. The sweat was dropping down my nose, so close was I running to the limit of my time.

"Suddenly there was a lurch, and I dived forward, ramming my head into the front of the cab, coming up with a rebound that landed me across the small of my back on the seat, and sent half of my pail of eggs helter-skelter over the floor.

"We had stopped. Here was Agassiz's house; and without taking time to pick up the eggs that were scattered, I jumped out with my pail and pounded at the door.

"No one was astir in the house. But I would stir someone. And I did. Right in the midst of the racket the door opened. It was the maid.

"'Agassiz,' I gasped, 'I want Professor Agassiz, quick!' And

I pushed by her into the hall.

"'Go 'way, sir. I'll call the police. Professor Agassiz is in bed. Go 'way, sir!'

"'Call him — Agassiz — instantly, or I'll call him myself.'

"But I didn't; for just then a door overhead was flung open, a great white-robed figure appeared on the dim landing above, and a quick loud voice called excitedly, —

"'Let him in! Let him in. I know him. He has my turtle eggs!'

"And the apparition, slipperless, and clad in anything but an academic gown, came sailing down the stairs.

"The maid fled. The great man, his arms extended, laid hold of me with both hands, and dragging me and my precious pail into his study, with a swift, clean stroke laid open one of the eggs, as the watch in my trembling hands ticked its way to seven as if nothing unusual were happening to the history of the world."

THE SEASON OF
SUMMER

R. BRUCE HORSFALL

THE WILD ANIMALS AT PLAY

The watcher of wild animals never gets used to the sight of their mirthless sport. In all other respects animal play is entirely human.

A great deal of human play is serious — desperately serious on the football-field, and at the card-table, as when a lonely player is trying to kill time with solitaire.

I have watched a great ungainly hippopotamus for hours trying to do the same solemn thing by cuffing a croquet-ball back and forth from one end of his cage to the other. His keepers told me that without the play-thing the poor caged giant would fret and worry himself to death. It was his game of solitaire.

In all their games of rivalry the animals are serious as humans, and, forgetting the fun, often fall to fighting — a sad case, indeed. But brutes are brutes. We cannot expect anything better of the animals. Only this morning the whole flock of chickens in the hen-yard started suddenly on the wild flap to see which would beat to the back fence and wound up on the "line" in a free fight, two of the cockerels tearing the feathers from each other in a desperate set-to.

You have seen puppies fall out in the same human fashion, and kittens also, and older folk as well. I have seen a game of wood-tag among friendly gray squirrels come to a finish in a fight. As the crows pass over during the winter afternoon, you will notice their play — racing each other through the air, diving, swooping, cawing in their fun, when suddenly someone's temper snaps, and there is a mix-up in the air.

They can get angry, but they cannot laugh. I once saw what I thought was a twinkle of merriment, however, in an elephant's eye. It was at the circus several years ago. The keeper had just set down for one of the elephants a bucket of water which a perspiring youth had brought in. The big beast sucked it quietly up, — the whole of it, — swung gently around; as if to thank the perspiring boy, then soused him, the whole bucketful! Everybody roared, and one of the other elephants joined in with trumpetings, so huge and jolly was the joke.

The elephant who played the trick looked solemn enough, except for a twitch at the lips and a glint in the eye. There is something of a smile about every elephant's lips, to be sure, and fun is so contagious that one should hesitate to say that he saw an elephant laugh. But if that elephant didn't laugh, it was not his fault.

From the elephant to the infusorian, the microscopic animal of a single cell known as the paramœcium, is a far cry — to the extreme opposite end of the animal kingdom, worlds apart. Yet I have seen *Paramœcium caudatum* at play in a drop of water under a compound microscope, as I have seen elephants at play in their big bath-tub at the zoological gardens.

Place a drop of stagnant water under your microscope and watch these atoms of life for yourself. Invisible to the naked eye, they are easily followed on the slide as they skate and whirl and chase one another to the boundaries of their playground and back again, first one of them "it," then another. They stop to eat, they slow up to divide their single-celled bodies into two cells, the two cells now two living creatures where a moment before they were but one, both of them swimming off immediately to feed and multiply and play.

Play seems to be as natural and as necessary to the wild animals as it is to human beings. Like us the animals play hardest while young, but as some human children never outgrow their youth and love of play, so there are old animals that never grow too fat nor too stiff nor too stupid to play.

The condition of the body has a great deal to do with the state of the spirit. The sleek, lithe otter could not possibly grow fat. He keeps in trim because he cannot help it, perhaps, but however that may be, he is a very boy for play, and even goes so far as to build himself a slide or chute for the fun of diving down it into the water. A writer in one of the magazines tells of an otter in the New York Zoological Park that swam and dived with a round stone balanced on his head,

Building a slide is more than we children used to do, for we had ready-made for us grandfather's two big slanting cellar-doors, down which we slid and slid and slid till the wood was scoured white and slippery with the sliding. The otter loves to slide. Up he climbs on the bank, then down he goes — splash — into the stream. Up he climbs and down he goes time after time, day after day. There is nothing like a slide, unless it is a cellar-door.

How much of a necessity to the otter is his play, one would like to know — what he would give up for it, and how he would do deprived of it. In the case of Pups, my neighbor's beautiful young collie, play seems more needful than food. There are no children, no one, to play with him there, so that the sight of my small boys sets him almost frantic.

His efforts to induce a hen or a rooster to play with him are pathetic. The hen cannot understand. She hasn't a particle of play in her anyhow, but Pups cannot get that through his head. He runs rapidly around her, drops on all fours flat, swings his tail, cocks his ears, looks appealingly and barks a few little cackle-barks, as nearly hen-like as he can bark them, then dashes off and whirls back while the hen picks up another bug. She never sees Pups. The old white coon cat is better; but she is usually up the miff-tree. Pups steps on her, knocks her over, or otherwise offends, especially when he tags her out into the fields and spoils her hunting. The Society for the Prevention of Cruelty to Animals ought to send some child or puppy out to play with Pups of a Saturday.

57

SUMMER

I doubt if among the lower forms of animals play holds any such prominent place as with the dog and the keen-witted, intelligent otter. To catch these lower animals at play is a rare experience. One of our naturalists describes the game of "follow my leader," as he watched it played by a school of minnows — a most unusual record, but not at all hard to believe, for I saw recently, from the bridge in the Boston Public Garden, a school of goldfish playing at something very much like it.

This naturalist was lying stretched out upon an old bridge, watching the minnows through a large crack between the planks, when he saw one leap out of the water over a small twig floating at the surface. Instantly another minnow broke the water and flipped over the twig, followed by another and another, the whole school, as so many sheep, or so many children, following the leader over the twig.

The love of play seems to be one of the elemental needs of all life above the plants, and the games of us human children seem to have been played before the dry land was, when there were only water babies in the world, for certainly the fish never learned "follow my leader" from us. Nor did my young bees learn from us their game of "prisoners' base" which they play almost every summer noontime in front of the hives. And what is the game the flies play about the cord of the drop-light in the centre of the kitchen ceiling?

One of the most interesting animal games that I ever saw was played by a flock of butterflies on the very top of Mount Hood, whose pointed snow-piled peak looks down from the clouds over the whole vast State of Oregon.

Mount Hood is an ancient volcano, eleven thousand two hundred twenty-five feet high. Some seven thousand feet or more up, we came to "Tie-up Rock" — the place on the climb where the glacier snows lay before us and we were tied up to one another and all of us fastened by rope to the guide.

From this point to the peak, it was sheer deep snow. For the last eighteen hundred feet we clung to a rope that was anchored on the edge of the crater at the summit, and cut our steps as we climbed.

Once we had gained the peak, we lay down behind a pile of sulphurous rock, out of the way of the cutting wind, and watched the steam float up from the crater, with the widest world in view that I ever turned my eyes upon.

The draft pulled hard about the openings among the rock-piles, but hardest up a flue, or chimney, that was left in the edge of the crater-rim where parts of the rock had fallen away.

As we lay at the side of this flue, we soon discovered that butterflies were hovering about us; no, not hovering, but flying swiftly up between the rocks from somewhere down the flue. I could scarcely believe my eyes. What could any living thing be doing here? — and of all things, butterflies? This was three or four thousand feet above the last vestige of vegetation, a mere point of volcanic rock (the jagged edge-piece of an old crater) wrapped in eternal ice and snow, with sulphurous gases pouring over it, and across it blowing a wind that would freeze as soon as the sun was out of the sky.

But here were real butterflies. I caught two or three of them and found them to be vanessas (*Vanessa californica*), a close relative of our mourning-cloak butterfly. They were all of one species, apparently, but what were they doing here?

Scrambling to the top of the piece of rock behind which I had been resting, I saw that the peak was alive with butterflies, and that they were flying — over my head, out down over the crater, and out of sight behind the peak, whence they reappeared, whirling up the flue past me on the wings of the draft that pulled hard through it, to sail down over the crater again, and again to be caught by the draft and pulled up the flue, to their evident delight, up and out over the peak, where they could again take wings, as boys take their sleds, and so down again for the fierce upward draft that bore them whirling over Mount Hood's pointed peak.

Here they were, thousands of feet above the snowline, where there was no sign of vegetation, where the heavy vapors made the air to smell, where the very next day a wild snowstorm wrapped its frozen folds about the peak — here they were, butterflies, playing, a host of them, like so many schoolboys on the first coasting snow!

FROM T WHARF TO FRANKLIN FIELD

Over and over I read the list of saints and martyrs on the wall across the street, thinking dully how men used to suffer for their religion, and how, nowadays, they suffer for their teeth. For I was reclining in a dentist's chair, blinking through the window at the Boston Public Library, seeing nothing, however, nothing but the tiles on the roof, and the names of Luther, Wesley, Wycliffe, graven on the granite wall, while the dentist burred inside of my cranium and bored down to my toes for nerves. So, at least, it seemed.

By and by my gaze wandered blankly off to the square patch of sky in sight above the roof. A black cloud was driving past in the wind away up there. Suddenly a white fleck swept into the cloud, careened, spread two wide wings against it, and rounded a circle. Then another and another, until eight herring gulls were soaring white against the sullen cloud in that little square of sky high over the roofs of Boston.

Was this the heart of a vast city? Could I be in a dentist's chair? There was no doubt about the chair; but how quickly the red-green roof of the Library became the top of some great cliff; the droning noise of traffic in the streets, the wash of waves against the rocks; and yonder on the storm-stained sky those wheeling wings, how like the winds of the ocean, and the raucous voices, how they seemed to fill all the city with the sweep and the sound of the sea!

Boston, Baltimore, New York, Philadelphia, Chicago, San Francisco — do you live in any one of them or in any other city? If you do, then you have a surprisingly good chance to watch the ways of wild things and even to come near to the heart of Nature. Not so good a chance, to be sure, as in the country; but the city is by no means so lacking in wild life or so shunned by the face of Nature as we commonly believe.

61

SUMMER

All great cities are alike, all of them very different, too, in details; Boston's streets, for instance, being crookeder than most, but like them all, reaching out for many a mile before they turn into country roads and lanes with borders of quiet and wide green fields.

But Boston has the wide waters of the Harbor and the Charles River Basin. And it also has T Wharf! They did not throw the tea overboard there, back in Revolutionary days, as you may be told, but T Wharf is famous, nevertheless, famous for fish!

Fish? Swordfish and red snappers, scup, shad, squid, squeteague, sharks, skates, smelts, sculpins, sturgeon, scallops; halibut, haddock, hake — to say nothing of mackerel, cod, and countless freak things caught by trawl and seine all the way from Boston Harbor to the Grand Banks! I have many a time sat on T Wharf and caught short, flat flounders with my line. It is almost as good as a trip to the Georges in the "We're Here" to visit T Wharf; and then to walk slowly up through Quincy Market. Surely no single walk in the woods will yield a tithe of the life to be found here, and found only here for us, brought as the fish and game and fruits have been from the ends of the earth and the depths of the sea.

There is no reason why city children should not know a great deal about animal life, nor why the teachers in city schools should feel that nature study is impossible for them. For, leaving the wharf with its fish and gulls and fleet of schooners, you come up four or five blocks to old King's Chapel Burying Ground where the Boston sparrows roost. Boston is full of interesting sights, but none more interesting to the bird-lover than this sparrow-roost. The great bird rocks in the Pacific, described in another chapter of this book,[4] are

---

[4] See "The Sea-Birds' Home," pp. 72-77.

larger, to be sure, yet hardly more clamorous when, in the dusk, the sparrow clans begin to gather; nor hardly wilder than this city roost when the night lengthens, and the quiet creeps down the alleys and along the empty streets, and the sea winds stop on the corners, and the lamps, like low-hung stars, light up the sleeping birds till their shadows waver large upon the stark walls about the old graveyard that break far overhead as rim rock breaks on the desert sky.

Now shift the scene to an early summer morning on Boston Common, two blocks farther up, and on to the Public Garden across Charles Street. There are more wild birds to be seen in the Garden on a May morning than there are here in the woods of Hingham, and the summer still finds some of them about the shrubs and pond. And it is an easy place in which to watch them. One of our bird-students has found over a hundred species in the Garden. Can any one say that the city offers a poor chance for nature-study? This is the story of every great city park. My friend Professor Herbert E. Walter found nearly one hundred and fifty species of birds in Lincoln Park, Chicago. And have you ever read Mr. Bradford Torrey's delightful essay called "Birds on Boston Common"?

Then there are the squirrels and the trees on the Common; the flowers, bees, butterflies, and even the schools of goldfish, in the pond of the Garden — enough of life, insect-life, plant-life, bird-life, fish-life, for more than a summer of lessons.

Nor is this all. One block beyond the Garden stands the Natural History Museum, crowded with mounted specimens of birds and beasts, reptiles, fishes, and shells beyond number, — more than you can study, perhaps. You city folk, instead of having too little, have altogether too much of too many things. But such a museum is always a suggestive place for one who loves the out-of-doors. And the more one knows of nature, the more one gets out of the museum. You can carry there, and often answer, the questions that come to you in your tramps afield, in your visits to the Garden, and in your reading of books. Then add to this the great Agassiz Museum at Harvard University, and the Aquarium at South Boston, and the Zöological Gardens at Franklin Park, and the Arnold Arboretum — all of these with their multitude of mounted specimens and their living forms for *you!* For me also; and in from the country I come, very often, to study natural history in the city.

What is true of Boston is true of every city in some degree. The sun and the moon and stars shine upon the city as upon the country, and during my years of city life (I lived in the very heart of Boston) it was my habit to climb to my roof, above the din and glare of the crowded street, and here among the chimney-pots to lie down upon my back, the city far below me, and overhead the blue sky, the Milky Way, the constellations, or the moon, swinging —

> "Through the heaven's wide pathless way,
> And oft, as if her head she bowed
> Stooping through a fleecy cloud."

Here, too, I have watched the gulls that sail over the Harbor, especially in the winter. From this outlook I have seen the winging geese pass over, and heard the faint calls of other migrating flocks, voices that were all the more mysterious for their falling through the muffling hum that rises from the streets and spreads over the wide roof of the city as a soft night wind over the peaked roofs of a forest of firs.

Strangely enough here on the roof I have watched the only nighthawks that I have ever found in Massachusetts. This is surely the last place you would expect to find such wild, spooky, dusk-loving creatures as nighthawks. Yet here, on the tarred and pebbled roofs, here among the whirling, squeaking, smoking chimney-pots, here above the crowded, noisy streets, these birds built their nests, — laid their eggs, rather, for they build no nests, — reared their young, and in the long summer twilight rose and fell through the smoky air, uttering their peevish cries and making their ghostly booming sounds with their high-diving, just as if they were out over the darkening swales along some gloomy swamp-edge.

For many weeks I had a big tame spider in the corner of my study there in that city flat, and I have yet to read an account of all the species of spiders to be found dwelling within the walls of any great city. Even Argiope of the meadows is doubtless found in the Fens. Not far away from my flat, down near the North Station, one of my friends on the roof of his flat kept several hives of bees. They fed on the flowers of the Garden, on those in dooryards, and on the honey-yielding lindens which stand here and there throughout the city. Pigeons and sparrows built their nests within sight of my windows; and by going early to the roof I could see the sun rise, and in the evening I could watch it go down behind the hills of Belmont as now I watch it from my lookout here on Mullein Hill.

One is never far from the sky, nor from the earth, nor from the free, wild winds, nor from the wilder night that covers city and sea and forest with its quiet, and fills them all with lurking shadows that never shall be tamed.

A CHAPTER OF THINGS TO HEAR THIS SUMMER

I

The fullness, the flood, of life has come, and, contrary to one's expectations, a marked silence has settled down over the waving fields and the cool deep woods. I am writing these lines in the lamplight, with all the windows and doors open to the dark July night. The summer winds are moving in the trees. A cricket and a few small green grasshoppers are chirping in the grass; but nothing louder is near at hand. And nothing louder is far off, except the cry of the whip-poor-will in the wood road. But him you hear in the spring and autumn as well as in the summer. Ah, listen! My tree-toad in the grapevine over the bulkhead door!

This is a voice you must hear — on cloudy summer days, toward twilight, and well into the evening. Do you know what it is to feel lonely? If you do, I think, then, that you know how the soft, far-off, eerie cry of the tree-toad sounds. He is prophesying rain, the almanac people think, but I think it is only the sound of rain in his voice, summer rain after a long drouth, cooling, reviving, soothing rain, with just a patter of something in it that I cannot describe, something that I used to hear on the shingles of the garret over the rafters where the bunches of horehound and catnip and pennyroyal hung.

II

You ought to hear the lively clatter of a mowing machine. It is hot out of doors; the roads are beginning to look dusty; the insects are tuning up in the grass, and, like their chorus all together, and marching round and round the meadow, moves the mower's whirring blade. I love the sound. Haying is hard, sweet work. The farmer who does not love his haying ought to be made to keep a country store and sell kerosene oil and lumps of dead salt pork out of a barrel. He could not appreciate a live, friendly pig.

Down the long swath sing the knives, the cogs click above the square corners, and the big, loud thing sings on again, — the song of "first-fruits," the first great ingathering of the season, — a song to touch the heart with joy and sweet solemnity.

III

You ought to hear the Katydids — two of them on the trees outside your window. They are not saying "Katy did," nor singing "Katy did"; they are fiddling "Katy did," "Katy didn't" — by rasping the fore wings.

Is the sound "Katy" or "Katy did"? or what is said? Count the notes. Are they at the rate of two hundred per minute? Watch the instrumentalist till you make sure it is the male who is wooing Katy with his persistent guitar. The male has no long ovipositors.

IV

Another instrumentalist to hear is the big cicada or "harvest-fly." There is no more characteristic sound of all the summer than his big, quick, startling whirr — a minute mowing-machine up on the limb overhead! Not so minute either, for the creature is fully two inches long, with bulging eyes and a click to his wings when he flies that can be heard a hundred feet away! "Dog-days-z-z-z-z-z-z-z" is the song he sings to me.

SUMMER

V

This is the season of small sounds. As a test of the keenness of your ears go out at night into some open glade in the woods or by the side of some pond and listen for the squeaking of the bats flitting and wavering above in the uncertain light over your head. You will need a stirless midsummer dusk; and if you can hear the thin, fine squeak as the creature dives near your head, you may be sure your ears are almost as keen as those of the fox. The sound is not audible to most human ears.

VI

Another set of small sounds characteristic of midsummer is the twittering of the flocking swallows in the cornfields and upon the telegraph-wires. This summer I have had long lines of the young birds and their parents from the old barn below the hill strung on the wires from the house across the lawn. Here they preen while some of the old birds hawk for flies, the whole line of them breaking into a soft little twitter each time a newcomer alights among them. One swallow does not make a summer, but your electric light wires sagging with them is the very soul of the summer.

VII

In the deep, still woods you will hear the soft call of the robin — a low, pensive, plaintive note unlike its spring cry or the after-shower song. It is as if the voice of the slumberous woods were speaking, — without alarm, reproach, or welcome either. It is an invitation to stretch yourself on the deep moss and let the warm shadows of the summer woods steal over you with sleep.

And this, too, is a thing to learn. Doing something, hearing something, seeing something by no means exhausts our whole business with the out-of-doors. To lie down and do nothing, to be able to keep silence and to rest on the great whirling globe is as needful as to know everything going on about us.

VIII

There is one bird-song so characteristic of mid summer that I think every lover of the woods must know it: the oft-repeated, the constant notes of the red-eyed vireo or "preacher." Wilson Flagg says of him: "He takes the part of a deliberative orator who explains his subject in a few words and then makes a pause for his hearers to reflect upon it. We might suppose him to be repeating moderately with a pause between each sentence, 'You see it — you know it — do you hear me? — do you believe it?' All these strains are delivered with a rising inflection at the close, and with a pause, as if waiting for an answer."

IX

A few other bird-notes that are associated with hot days and stirless woods, and that will be worth your hearing are the tree-top song of the scarlet tanager. He is one of the summer sights, a dash of the burning tropics is his brilliant scarlet and jet black, and his song is a loud, hoarse, rhythmical carol that has the flame of his feathers in it and the blaze of the sun. You will know it from the cool, liquid song of the robin both by its peculiar quality and because it is a short song, and soon ended, not of indefinite length like the robin's.

Then the peculiar, coppery, reverberating, or *confined* song of the indigo bunting — as if the bird were singing inside some great kettle.

One more — among a few others — the softly falling,

round, small, upward-swinging call of the wood pewee. Is it sad? Yes, sad. But sweeter than sad, restful, cooling, and inexpressibly gentle. All day long from high above your head and usually quite out of view, the voice — it seems hardly a voice — breaks the long silence of the summer woods.

X

When night comes down with the long twilight there sounds a strange, almost awesome *quawk* in the dusk over the fields. It sends a thrill through me, notwithstanding its nightly occurrence all through July and August. It is the passing of a pair of night herons — the black-crowned, I am sure, although this single pair only fly over. Where the birds are numerous they nest in great colonies.

It is the wild, eerie *quawk* that you should hear, a far-off, mysterious, almost uncanny sound that fills the twilight with a vague, untamed something, no matter how bright and civilized the day may have been.

XI

From the harvest fields comes the sweet whistle of Bob White, the clear, round notes rolling far through the hushed summer noon; in the wood-lot the crows and jays have already begun their cawings and screamings that later on become the dominant notes of the golden autumn. They are not so loud and characteristic now because of the insect orchestra throbbing with a rhythmic beat through the air. So wide, constant, and long-continued is this throbbing note of the insects that by midsummer you almost cease to notice it. But stop and listen — field crickets, katydids, long-horned grasshoppers, snowy tree-crickets: *chwi-chwi-chwi-chwi* — *thrr-r-r-r-r-r* — *crrri-crrri-*

crrri-crrri — *gru-gru-gru-gru* – *retreat-retreat-retreat-treat-treat* — like the throbbing the pulse.

XII

One can do no more than suggest in a short chapter like this; and all that I am doing here is catching for you some of the still, small voices of *my* summer. How unlike those of your summer they may be I can easily imagine, for you are in the Pacific Coast, or off on the vast prairies of Canada, or down in the sunny fields and hill-country of the South.

I have done enough if I have suggested that you stop and listen; for after all it is having ears which hear *not* that causes the trouble. Hear the voices that make your summer vocal — the loud and still voices which alike pass unheeded unless we pause to hear.

As a lesson in listening, go out some quiet evening, and as the shadows slip softly over the surface of the wood-walled pond, listen to the breathing of the fish as they come to the top, and the splash of the muskrats, or the swirl of the pickerel as he ploughs a furrow through the silence.

THE SEA-BIRDS' HOME

After my wandering for years among the quiet lanes and along the winding cow-paths of the home fields, my trip to the wild-bird rocks in the Pacific Ocean, as you can imagine, was a thrilling experience. We chartered a little launch at Tillamook, and, after a fight of hours and hours to cross Tillamook Bar at the mouth of the bay, we got out upon the wide Pacific, and steamed down the coast for Three-Arch Rocks, which soon began to show far ahead of us just off the rocky shore.[5]

I had never been on the Pacific before, nor had I ever before seen the birds that were even now beginning to dot the sea and to sail over and about us as we steamed along. It was all new, so new that the very water of the Pacific looked unlike the familiar water of the Atlantic. And surely the waves were different, longer, grayer, smoother, with an immensely mightier heave. At least they seemed so, for every time we rose on the swell, it was as if our boat were in the hand of Old Ocean, and his mighty arm were "putting" us, as the athlete "puts" the shot. It was all new and strange and very wild to me, with the wild cries of the sea-birds already beginning to reach us as flocks of the birds passed around and over our heads.

The fog was lifting. The thick, wet drift that had threatened our little launch on Tillamook Bar stood clear of the shouldering sea to the westward, and in over the shore, like an upper sea, hung at the fir-girt middles of the mountains, as level and as

---

[5] Today the site of Three Arch Rocks is a national wildlife refuge. To prevent disturbance to the seabirds, the refuge is closed to public entry year-round; waters within 500 feet of the refuge are closed to all watercraft from May 1st through September 15th. The Three Arch Rocks can best be viewed from the mainland at Cape Meares and in the town of Oceanside, Oregon.

gray as the sea below. There was no breeze. The long, smooth swell of the Pacific swung under us and in, until it whitened at the base of the three rocks that rose out of the sea in our course, and that now began to take on form in the foggy distance. Gulls were flying over us, lines of black cormorants and crowds of murres were winging past, but we were still too far away from the looming rocks to see that the gray of their walls was the gray of uncounted colonies of nesting birds, colonies that covered their craggy steeps as, on shore, the green firs clothed the slopes of the Coast Range Mountains up to the hanging fog.

As we ran on nearer, the sound of the surf about the rocks became audible, the birds in the air grew more numerous, their cries now faintly mingling with the sound of the sea. A hole in the side of the middle Rock, a mere fleck of foam it seemed at first, widened rapidly into an arching tunnel through which our boat might run; the swell of the sea began to break over half-sunken ledges; and soon upon us fell the damp shadows of the three great rocks, for now we were looking far up at their sides, where we could see the birds in their guano-gray rookeries, rookery over rookery, — gulls, cormorants, guillemots, puffins, murres, — encrusting the sides from tide-line to pinnacles, as the crowding barnacles encrusted the bases from the tide-line down.

We had not approached without protest, for the birds were coming off to meet us, wheeling and clacking overhead, the nearer we drew, in a constantly thickening cloud of lowering wings and tongues. The clamor was indescribable, the tossing flight enough to make one mad with the motion of wings. The air was filled, thick, with the whirling and the screaming, the clacking, the honking, close to our ears, and high up in the peaks, and far out over the waves. Never had I been in this world before. Was I on my earth? or had I suddenly wakened up in some old sea world where there was no dry land, no life but this?

We rounded the outer or Shag Rock and headed slowly in opposite the yawning hole of the middle Rock as into some mighty cave, so sheer and shadowy rose the walls above us, — so like to cavern thunder was the throbbing of the surf through the hollow arches, was the flapping and screaming of the birds against the high circling walls, was the deep, menacing grumble of the bellowing sea-lions, as, through the muffle of surf and sea-fowl, herd after herd lumbered headlong into the foam.

It was a strange, wild scene. Hardly a mile from the Oregon coast, but cut off by breaker and bar from the abrupt, uninhabited shore, the three rocks of the Reservation, each pierced with its resounding arch, heaved their huge shoulders from the waves straight up, high, towering, till our little steamer coasted their dripping sides like some puffing pygmy.

Each rock was perhaps as large as a solid city square and as high as the tallest of sky-scrapers; immense, monstrous piles, each of them, and run through by these great caverns or arches, dim, dripping, filled with the noise of the waves and the beat of thousands of wings.

They were of no part or lot with the dry land. Their wave-scooped basins were set with purple starfish and filled with green and pink anemones, and beaded many deep with mussels of amethyst and jet that glittered in the clear beryl waters; and, above the jeweled basins, like fabled beasts of old, lay the sea-lions, uncouth forms, flippered, reversed in shape, with throats like the caves of Aeolus, hollow, hoarse, discordant; and higher up, on every jutting bench and shelf, in every weathered rift, over every jog of the ragged cliffs, to their bladed backs and pointed peaks, swarmed the sea-birds, webfooted, amphibious, shaped of the waves, with stormy voices given them by the winds that sweep in from the sea.

74

SUMMER

As I looked up at the amazing scene, at the mighty rocks and the multitude of winging forms, I seemed to see three swirling piles of life, three cones that rose like volcanoes from the ocean, their sides covered with living lava, their craters clouded with the smoke of wings, while their bases seemed belted by the rumble of a multi-throated thunder. The very air was dank with the smell of strange, strong volcanic gases, — no breath of the land, no odor of herb, no scent of fresh soil; but the raw, rank smells of rookery and saline, kelpy, fetid; the stench of fish and bedded guano, and of the reeking pools where the sea-lion herds lay sleeping on the lower rocks in the sun.

A boat's keel was beneath me, but as I stood out on the pointed prow, barely above the water, and found myself thrust forward without will or effort among the crags and caverns, among the shadowy walls, the damps, the smells, the sounds, among the bellowing beasts in the churning waters about me, and into the storm of wings and tongues in the whirling air above me, I passed from the things I had known, and the time and the earth of man, into a monstrous period of the past.

This was the home of the sea-birds. Amid all the din we landed from a yawl and began our climb toward the top of Shag Rock, the outermost of the three. And here we had another and a different sight of the wild life. It covered every crag. I clutched it in my hands; I crushed it under my feet; it was thick in the air about me. My narrow path up the face of the rock was a succession of sea-bird rookeries, of crowded eggs, and huddled young, hairy or naked or wet from the shell. Every time my fingers felt for a crack overhead they touched something warm that rolled or squirmed; every time my feet moved under me, for a hold, they pushed in among top-shaped eggs that turned on the shelf or went over far below; and whenever I hugged the pushing wall I must bear off from a mass of squealing, struggling, shapeless things, just hatched. And down upon me, as rookery after rookery of old birds whirred in fright from their ledges, fell crashing eggs and unfledged young, that the greedy gulls devoured ere they touched the sea.

I was midway in the climb, at a bad turn round a point, edging inch by inch along, my face pressed against the hard face of the rock, my feet and fingers gripping any crack or seam they could feel, when out of the deep space behind me I caught the swash of waves. Instantly a cold hand seemed to clasp me from behind.

I flattened against the rock, my whole body, my very mind clinging desperately for a hold, — a falling fragment of shale, a gust of wind, the wing-stroke of a frightened bird, enough to break the hold and swing me out over the water, washing faint and far below. A long breath, and I was climbing again.

We were on the outer Rock, our only possible ascent taking us up the sheer south face. With the exception of an occasional Western gull's and pigeon guillemot's nest, these steep sides were occupied entirely by the California murres, penguin-shaped birds about the size of a small wild duck, chocolate-brown above, with white breasts, — which literally covered the sides of the three great rocks wherever they could find a hold. If a million meant anything, I should say there were a million murres nestling on this outer Rock; not nesting either, for the egg is laid upon the bare ledge, as you might place it upon a mantel, — a single sharp-pointed egg, as large as a turkey's, and just as many of them on the ledge as there is standing-room for the birds. The murre broods her very large egg by standing straight up over it, her short legs, by dint of stretching, allowing her to straddle it, her short tail propping her securely from behind.

On, up along the narrow back, or blade, of the rock, and

over the peak, were the well-spaced nests of the Brandt's cormorants, nests the size of an ordinary straw hat, made of sea-grass and the yellow-flowered sulphur-weed that grew in a dense mat over the north slope of the top, each nest holding four long, dirty blue eggs or as many black, shivering young; and in the low sulphur-weed, all along the roof-like slope of the top, built the gulls and the tufted puffins; and, with the burrowing puffins, often in the same holes, were found the Kaeding's petrels; while down below them, as up above them, — all around the rock-rim that dropped sheer to the sea, — stood the cormorants, black, silent, statuesque; and everywhere were nests and eggs and young, and everywhere were flying, crying birds — above, about, and far below me, a whirling, whirring vortex of wings that had caught me in its funnel.

THE MOTHER MURRE

I hear the bawling of my neighbor's cow. Her calf was carried off yesterday, and since then, during the long night, and all day long, her insistent woe has made our hillside melancholy. But I shall not hear her tonight, not from this distance. She will lie down tonight with the others of the herd, and munch her cud. Yet, when the rattling stanchions grow quiet and sleep steals along the stalls, she will turn her ears at every small stirring; she will raise her head to listen and utter a low, tender *moo*. Her full udder hurts; but her cud is sweet. She is only a cow.

Had she been a wild cow, or had she been out with her calf in a wild pasture, the mother-love in her would have lived for six months. Here in the barn she will be forced to forget her calf in a few hours, and by morning her mother-love shall utterly have died.

There is a mother-principle alive in all nature that never dies. This is different from mother-love. The oak tree responds to the mother-principle, and bears acorns. It is a law of life. The mother-love or passion, on the other hand, occurs only among the higher animals. It is very common; and yet, while it is one of the strongest, most interesting, most beautiful of animal traits, it is at the same time the most individual and variable of all animal traits.

This particular cow of my neighbor's that I hear lowing, is an entirely gentle creature ordinarily, but with a calf at her side she will pitch at any one who approaches her. And there is no other cow in the herd that mourns so long after her calf. The mother in her is stronger, more enduring, than in any of the other nineteen cows in the barn. My own cow hardly mourns at all when her calf is taken away. She might be an oak tree losing its acorns, or a crab losing her hatching eggs, so far as any show of love is concerned.

SUMMER

The female crab attaches her eggs to her swimmerets and carries them about with her for their protection as the most devoted of mothers; yet she is no more conscious of them, and feels no more for them, than the frond of a cinnamon fern feels for its spores. She is a mother, without the love of the mother.

In the spider, however, just one step up the animal scale from the crab, you find the mother-love or passion. Crossing a field the other day, I came upon a large female spider of the hunter family, carrying a round white sack of eggs, half the size of a cherry, attached to her spinnerets. Plucking a long stem of grass, I detached the sack of eggs without bursting it. Instantly the mother turned and sprang at the grass-stem, fighting and biting until she got to the sack, which she seized in her strong jaws and made off with as fast as her long, rapid legs would carry her.

I laid the stem across her back and again took the sack away. She came on for it, fighting more fiercely than before. Once more she seized it; once more I forced it from her jaws, while she sprang at the grass-stem and tried to tear it to pieces. She must have been fighting for two minutes when, by a regrettable move on my part, one of her legs was injured. She did not falter in her fight. On she rushed for the sack as fast as I pulled it away. She would have fought for that sack, I believe, until she had not one of her eight legs to stand on, had I been cruel enough to compel her. It did not come to this, for suddenly the sack burst, and out poured, to my amazement, a myriad of tiny brown spiderlings. Before I could think what to do that mother spider had rushed among them and caused them to swarm upon her, covering her, many deep, even to the outer joints of her long legs. I did not disturb her again, but stood by and watched her slowly move off with her encrusting family to a place of safety.

I had seen these spiders try hard to escape with their egg-sacks before, but had never tested the strength of their purpose. For a time after this experience I made a point of taking the sacks away from every spider I found. Most of them scurried off to seek their own safety; one of them dropped her sack of her own accord; some of them showed reluctance to leave it; some of them a disposition to fight; but none of them the fierce, consuming mother-fire of the one with the hurt leg.

Among the fishes, much higher animal forms than the spiders, we find the mother-love only in the *males*. It is the male stickleback that builds the nest, then goes out and *drives* the female in to lay her eggs, then straightway drives her out to prevent her eating them, then puts himself on guard outside the nest to protect them from other sticklebacks and other enemies, until the young shall hatch and be able to swim away by themselves. Here he stays for a month, without eating or sleeping, so far as we know.

It is the male toadfish that crawls into the nest-hole and takes charge of the numerous family. He may dig the hole, too, as the male stickleback builds the nest. I do not know as to that. But I have raised many a stone in the edge of the tide along the shore of Naushon Island in Buzzard's Bay, to find the under surface covered with round, drop-like, amber eggs, and in the shallow cavity beneath, an old male toadfish, slimy and croaking, and with a countenance ugly enough to turn a prowling eel to stone. The female deposits the eggs, glues them fast with much nicety to the under surface of the rock, as a female might, and finishes her work. Departing at once, she leaves the coming brood to the care of the male, who from this time, without relief or even food in all probability, assumes the role and all the responsibilities of mother, and must consequently feel all the mother-love.

Something like this is true of the common hornpout, or catfish, I believe, though I have never seen it recorded, and lack the chance at present of proving my earlier observations. I think it is father catfish that takes charge of the brood, of the swarm of kitten catfish, from the time the spawn is laid.

A curious sharing of mother qualities by male and female is shown in the Surinam toads of South America, where the male, taking the newly deposited eggs, places them upon the back of the female. Here, glued fast by their own adhesive jelly, they are soon surrounded by cells grown of the skin of the back, each cell capped by a lid. In these cells the eggs hatch, and the young go through their metamorphoses, apparently absorbing some nourishment through the skin of their mother. Finally they break through the lids of their cells and hop away. They might as well be toadstools upon a dead stump, so far as motherly care or concern goes, for, aside from allowing the male to spread the eggs upon her back, she is no more a mother to them than the dead stump is to the toadstools. She is host only to the little parasites.

I do not know of any mother-love among the reptiles. The mother-passion, so far as my observation goes, plays no part whatever in the life of reptiles. Whereas, passing on to the birds, the mother-passion becomes by all odds the most interesting thing in bird-life.

And is not the mother-passion among the mammals even more interesting? It is as if the watcher in the woods went out to see the mother animal only. It is her going and coming that we follow; her faring, foraging, and watch-care that let us deepest into the secrets of wild animal life.

On one of the large estates here in Hingham, a few weeks ago, a fox was found to be destroying poultry. The time of the raids, and their boldness, were proof enough that the fox must be a female with young. Poisoned meat was prepared for her, and at once the raids ceased. A few days later one of the workmen of the estate came upon the den of a fox, at the mouth of which lay dead a whole litter of young ones. They had been poisoned. The mother had not eaten the prepared food herself, but, had carried it home to her family. They must have died in the burrow, for it was evident from the signs that she had dragged them into the fresh air to revive them, and deposited them gently on the sand by the hole. Then in her perplexity she had brought various tidbits of mouse and bird and rabbit, which she placed at their noses to tempt them to wake up out of their strange sleep and eat. No one knows how long she watched beside the lifeless forms, nor what her emotions were. She must have left the neighborhood soon after, however, for no one has seen her since about the estate.

The bird mother is the bravest, tenderest, most appealing thing one ever comes upon in the fields. It is the rare exception, but we sometimes find the real mother wholly lacking among the birds, as in the case of our notorious cowbird, who sneaks about, watching her chance, when some smaller bird is gone, to drop her egg into its nest. The egg must be laid, the burden of the race has been put upon the bird, but not the precious burden of the child. She lays eggs; but is not a mother.

The same is true of the European cuckoos, but not quite true, in spite of popular belief, of our American cuckoos. For our birds (both species) build rude, elementary nests as a rule, and brood their eggs. Occasionally they may use a robin's or a catbird's nest, in order to save labor. So undeveloped is the mother in the cuckoo that if you touch her eggs she will leave them — abandon her rude nest and eggs as if any excuse were excuse enough for an escape from the cares of motherhood. How should a bird with so little mother-love ever learn to build a firm-walled, safe, and love-lined nest?

The great California condor is a most faithful and anxious mother; the dumb affection of both parent birds, indeed, for their single offspring is pathetically human. On the other hand, the mother in the turkey buzzard is so evenly balanced against the vulture in her that I have known a brooding bird to be so upset by the sudden approach of a man as to rise from off her eggs and devour them instantly, greedily, and make off on her serenely soaring wings into the clouds.

Such mothers, however, are not the rule. The buzzard, the cuckoo, and the cowbird are the striking exceptions. The flicker will keep on laying eggs as fast as one takes them from the nest-hole, until she has no more eggs to lay. The quail will sometimes desert her nest if even a single egg is so much as touched, but only because she knows that she has been discovered and must start a new nest, hidden in some new place, for safety. She is a wise and devoted mother, keeping her brood with her as a "covey" all winter long.

One of the most striking cases of mother-love which has ever come under my observation, I saw in the summer of 1912 on the bird rookeries of the Three-Arch Rocks Reservation off the coast of Oregon.

We were making our slow way toward the top of the outer rock. Through rookery after rookery of birds we climbed until we reached the edge of the summit. Scrambling over this edge, we found ourselves in the midst of a great colony of nesting murres — hundreds of them — covering this steep rocky part of the top.

As our heads appeared above the rim, many of the colony took wing and whirred over us out to sea, but most of them sat close, each bird upon its egg or over its chick, loath to leave, and so expose to us the hidden treasure. The top of the rock was somewhat cone-shaped, and in order to reach the peak and the colonies on the west side we had to make our way through this rookery of the murres. The first step among them, and the whole colony was gone, with a rush of wings and feet that sent several of the top-shaped eggs, rolling, and several of the young birds toppling over the cliff to the pounding waves and ledges far below.

We stopped, but the colony, almost to a bird, had bolted, leaving scores of eggs and scores of downy young squealing and running together for shelter, like so many beetles under a lifted board.

But the birds had not every one bolted, for here sat two of the colony among the broken rocks. These two had not been frightened off. That both of them were greatly alarmed, any one could see from their open beaks, their rolling eyes, their tense bodies on tiptoe for flight. Yet here they sat, their wings out like props, or more like gripping hands, as if they were trying to hold themselves down to the rocks against their wild desire to fly.

And so they were, in truth, for under their extended wings I saw little black feet moving. Those two mother murres were not going to forsake their babies! No, not even for these approaching monsters, such as they had never before seen, clambering over their rocks.

What was different about these two? They had their young ones to protect. Yes, but so had every bird in the great colony its young one, or its egg, to protect, yet all the others had gone. Did these two have more mother-love than the others? And hence, more courage, more intelligence?

We took another step toward them, and one of the two birds sprang into the air, knocking her baby over and over with the stroke of her wing, and coming within an inch of hurling it across the rim to be battered on the ledges below. The other bird raised her wings to follow, then clapped them back over her baby. Fear is the most contagious thing in the world; and that flap of fear by the other bird thrilled her, too, but as she had withstood the stampede of the colony, so she caught herself again and held on.

84

SUMMER

She was now alone on the bare top of the rock, with ten thousand circling birds screaming to her in the air above, and with two men creeping up to her with a big black camera that clicked ominously. She let the multitude scream, and with threatening beak watched the two men come on. A motherless baby, spying her, ran down the rock squealing for his life. She spread a wing, put her bill behind him and shoved him quickly in out of sight with her own baby. The man with the camera saw the act, for I heard his machine click, and I heard him say something under his breath that you would hardly expect a mere man and a game-warden to say. But most men have a good deal of the mother in them and the old bird had acted with such decision, such courage, such swift, compelling instinct, that any man, short of the wildest savage, would have felt his heart quicken at the sight.

"Just how compelling might that mother-instinct be?" I wondered. "Just how much would that mother-love stand?" I had dropped to my knees, and on all fours had crept up within about three feet of the bird. She still had chance for flight. Would she allow me to crawl any nearer? Slowly, very slowly, I stretched forward on my hands, like a measuring-worm, until my body lay flat on the rocks, and my fingers were within three inches of her. But her wings were twitching, a wild light danced in her eyes, and her head turned toward the sea.

For a whole minute I did not stir. I was watching — and the wings again began to tighten about the babies, the wild light in the eyes died down, the long, sharp beak turned once more toward me.

Then slowly, very slowly, I raised my hand, touched her feathers with the tip of one finger — with two fingers — with my whole hand, while loud camera click-clacked, click-clacked hardly four feet away!

It was a thrilling moment. I was not killing anything. I had no long-range rifle in my hands, coming up against the wind toward an unsuspecting creature hundreds of yards away. This was no wounded leopard charging me; no mother-bear defending with her giant might a captured cub. It was only a mother-bird, the size of a wild duck, with swift wings at her command, hiding under those wings her own and another's young, and her own boundless fear!

For the second time in my life I had taken captive with my bare hands a free wild bird. No, I had not taken her captive. She had made herself a captive; she had taken herself in the strong net of her mother-love.

And now her terror seemed quite gone. At the first touch of my hand I think she felt the love restraining it, and without fear or fret she let me reach under her and pull out the babies. But she reached after them with her bill to tuck them back out of sight, and when I did not let them go, she sidled toward me, quacking softly, a language that I perfectly understood, and was quick to respond to. I gave them back, fuzzy and black and white. She got them under her, stood up over them, pushed her wings down hard around them, her stout tail down, hard behind them, and together with them pushed in an abandoned egg that was close at hand. Her own baby, some one else's baby, and some one else's forsaken egg! She could cover no more; she had not feathers enough. But she had heart enough; and into her mother's heart she had already tucked every motherless egg and nestling of the thousands of frightened birds, screaming and wheeling in the air high over her head.

THE SEASON OF
AUTUMN

THE MUSKRATS ARE BUILDING

We have had a week of almost unbroken rain, and the water is standing over the swampy meadow. It is a dreary stretch, — this wet, sedgy land in the cold twilight, — drearier than any part of the woods or the upland pastures. They are empty; but the meadow is flat and wet, it is naked and all unsheltered. And a November night is falling.

The darkness deepens. A raw wind is rising. At nine o'clock the moon swings round and full to the crest of the ridge, and pours softly over. I button my heavy ulster close, and in my rubber boots go down to the stream and follow it out to the middle of the meadow, where it meets the main ditch. There is a sharp turn here toward the swamp; and here at the bend, behind a clump of black alders, I sit quietly down and wait.

I have come out to the bend to watch the muskrats building; for that small mound up the ditch is not an old haycock, but a half-finished muskrat house.

As I wait, the moon climbs higher over the woods. The water on the meadow shivers in the light. The wind bites through my heavy coat and drives me back, but not before I have seen one, two, three little creatures scaling the walls of the house with loads of mud-and-reed mortar. I am driven back by the cold, but not before I know that here in the desolate meadow is being rounded off a lodge, thick-walled and warm, and proof against the longest, bitterest of winters.

This is near the end of November. My fire-wood is in the cellar; I am about ready to put on the double-windows and the storm-doors. The muskrats are even now putting on theirs, for their house is all but finished. Winter is at hand: but we are prepared, the muskrats and I.

Throughout the summer the muskrats had no house, only their tunnels into the sides of the ditch, their roadways out into the grass, and their beds under the tussocks or among the roots of the old stumps. All those months the water was low in the ditch, and the beds among the tussocks were safe and

88

dry enough.

Now the November rains have filled river and ditch, flooded the tunnels, and crept up into the beds under the tussocks. Even a muskrat will creep out of his bed when cold, wet water creeps in. What shall he do for shelter? He knows. And long before the rains begin, he picks out the place for a house. He does not want to leave his meadow, therefore the only thing to do is to build, — move from under the tussock out upon the top of the tussock; and here, in its deep, wiry grass, make a new bed high and dry above the rising water; and close this new bed in with walls that circle and dome, and defy the very winter.

Such a house will require a great deal of work to build. Why should not two or three muskrats combine — make the house big enough to hold them all, save labor and warmth, too, and, withal, live sociably together? So they left, each one his single bed, and, joining efforts, started, about the middle of October, to build this winter house.

Slowly, night after night, the domed walls have been rising, although for several nights at a time I could see no apparent progress with the work. The builders were in no hurry. The cold was far off. But it is coming, and to-night it feels near and keen. And to-night there is no loafing about the lodge.

When this house is done, when the last hod of mud plaster has been laid on, — then the rains may descend and the floods come, but it will not fall. It is built upon a tussock; and a tussock — did you ever try to pull up a tussock?

Winter may descend, and boys and foxes may come — and they will come, but not before the walls are frozen. Then, let them come. The house will stand. It is boy-proof, almost; it is entirely rain-, cold-, and fox-proof. I have often seen where the fox has gone round and round the house in the snow, and where, at places, he has attempted to dig into the frozen mortar. But it was a foot thick, as hard as flint, and utterly impossible for his pick and shovel.

I said the floods, as well as the fox, may come. So they may, ordinarily; but along in March, when one comes as a freshet and rises to the dome of the house, then it fills the bed-chamber to the ceiling and drowns the dwellers out. I remember a freshet once in the end of February that flooded Lupton's Pond and drove the muskrats of the whole pond village to their ridgepoles, to the bushes, and to whatever wreckage the waters brought along.

> "The best-laid schemes o' mice and men
> Gang aft agley"

— and of muskrats, too.

But not very often do the muskrats' plans go thus agley. For muskrats and wood mice and birds and bees, and even the very trees of the forest, have a kind of natural foresight. They all look ahead, at the approach of autumn, and begin to provide against the coming cold. Yet, weather-wise as a muskrat may be, still he cannot know all that may happen; he cannot be ready for everything. And so, if now and then, he should prove foresight to be vain, he only shows that his plans and our plans, his life and our lives, are very much alike.

Usually, however, the muskrat's plans work out as he would have them. His foresight proves to be equal to all that the winter can bring. On the coldest winter days I shall look out over the bleak white waste to where his house shows, a tiny mound in the snow, and think of him safe and warm inside, as safe and warm as I am, in my house, here on the hilltop.

Indeed, I think the muskrat will be the warmer; for my big house here on Mullein Hill is sometimes cold. And the wind! If only I could drive the winter wind away from the corners of the house! But the house down in the meadow has no corners.

AUTUMN

It has walls, mud walls, so thick and round that the shrieking wind sweeps past unheard by the dwellers within; and all un-heeded the cold creeps over and over the low thatch, to crawl back and stiffen upon the meadow.

The doors of this meadow house swing wide open; through-out the winter; for they are in the bottom of the house, beneath the water, where only the muskrat can enter. Just outside the doors, down under the water and the roof of ice that covers all the flooded meadow are fresh calamus roots, and iris and arum — food in abundance, no matter how long the winter lasts.

No, the winter has not yet come; but it is coming, for the muskrats are building. Let it come. Let the cold crawl stiff and gray across the meadow. Let the whirling snow curl like smoke about the pointed top of the little tepee down by the meadow ditch. Let the north wind do its worst. For what care the dwell-ers in that thick-walled lodge beneath the snow? Down under the water their doors are open; their roadways up the ditches as free as in the summer; and the stems of the sedges just as juicy and pink and tender.

The muskrats are building. The buds are leaving. Winter is coming. I must get out my own storm-windows and double-doors; for even now a fire is blazing cheerily on my wide, warm hearth.

AN OUTDOOR LESSON

I have had many a person ask me, "What is the best way to learn about the out of doors ?" and I always answer, "Don't try to learn *about* it, but first go out of the house and get into the out of doors. Then open both eyes, use both of your ears, and stand in one place stock still as long as you can; and you will soon know the out of doors itself, which is better than knowing about it."

"But," says my learner, "if I go out of the house, I don't get into the out of doors at all, but into a city street!"

Look there — in the middle of the street! What is it? An English sparrow? Yes, an English sparrow, — six English sparrows. Are they not a part of the out of doors? And look up there, over your head — a strip of sky? Yes — is not a strip of blue sky a part of the out of doors?

Now let me tell you how I learned an outdoor lesson one night along a crowded city street.

It was a cold, wet night; and the thick, foggy twilight, settling down into the narrow streets, was full of smoke and smell and chill. A raw wind blew in from the sea and sent a shiver past every corner. The street lights blinked, the street mud glistened, the street noises clashed and rattled, and the street crowds poured up and down and bore me alone with them.

I was homesick — homesick for the country. I longed to hear the sound of the wind in the pine trees; I longed to hear the single far-away bark of the dog on the neighboring farm, or the bang of a barn door, or the clack of a guinea going to roost. It was half-past five, and thousands of clerks were pouring from the closing stores; but I was lonely, homesick for the quiet, the wideness, the trees and sky of the country.

Feeling thus, and seeing only the strange faces all about me, and the steep narrow walls of the street high above me, I drifted along, until suddenly I caught the sound of bird voices shrill and sharp through the din.

I stopped, but was instantly jostled out of the street, up against a grim iron fence, to find myself peering through the pickets into an ancient cemetery in the very heart of Boston.

As I looked, there loomed up in the fog and rain overhead the outlines of three or four gaunt trees, whose limbs were as thick with sparrows as they had ever been with leaves. A sparrow roost! Birds, ten thousand birds, gone to roost in the business section of a great city, with ten thousand human beings passing under them as they slept!

I got in behind a big waste-barrel by the iron fence and let the crowd surge past. It was such a sight as I had never seen. I had seen thousands of chimney swallows go to roost in the deserted chimneys of a great country house; I had many a time gone down at night to the great crow-roost in the pines at Cubby Hollow; but I had never stumbled upon a bird-roost on a crowded city street before!

The hurrying throng behind me thinned and straggled while I waited, watching by the iron fence. The wind freshened, the mist thickened into fine rain that came slanting down through the half-lighted trees; the sleeping sparrows twittered and shifted uneasily on the limbs.

The streets were being deserted. It was going to be a wild night on the water, and a wild night in the swaying, creaking tops of these old elm trees. I shivered at the thought of the sparrows sleeping out in such a night as this, and turned away toward my own snug roost hardly two blocks away.

The night grew wilder. The wind rattled down our street past a hundred loose shutters; the rain slapped against the windows, and then stopped as a heavy gust curled over the line of roofs opposite. I thought of the sparrows. Had they been driven from the tossing limbs? Could they cling fast in such a wind, and could they sleep?

Going to the window I looked down into the street. Only the electric light at the corner showed through the blur of the storm. The street was empty.

I slipped into my coat and went out; not even a policeman was in sight. Only the whirling sheets of rain, only the wild sounds of the wind were with me. The lights flared, but only to fill the streets with fantastic shadows and to open up a yawning cavern in every deep, dark doorway.

Keeping in the lee of the shuttered buildings, I made my way to the sparrow roost. I shall never forget the sight! Not a sparrow had left his perch, but every bird had now turned, facing the wind — breasting the wind, I should say; for every head was under a wing, as near as I could make out, and every breast was toward the storm. Here, on the limbs, as close as beads on a string, they clung and rocked in the arms of the wind, every one with his feathers tight to his body, his tail lying out flat on the storm.

Now there is the outdoor lesson I learned, and that is how I learned it. And what was the lesson? Why, this: that you are not shut away from Nature even in the heart of a great city; that the out of doors lies very close about you, as you hurry down a crowded city street.

LEAFING

No you never went "leafing" — not unless you are simon-pure country-bred. You do not know what the word means. You cannot find it in the unabridged dictionary — not in the sense in which I am using it. But there are many good words we country people use that are not, perhaps, in the dictionary.

And what do I mean by "leafing"? Get down that bundle of meal sacks, hitch into the one-horse hay-rig, throw in the rakes, and come. We are going into the woods for pig-bedding, for leaves to keep the pigs dry and warm this winter!

You never went after leaves for the pigs? Perhaps you never even had a pig. But a pig is worth having, if only to see the comfort he takes in the big bed of dry leaves you give him in the sunny corner of his pen. And if leafing had no other reward, the thought of the snoozing, snoring pig buried to his winking snout in the bed, would give joy and zest enough to the labor.

But leafing, like every other humble labor, has its own rewards, not the least of them being the leaves themselves and the getting of them!

We jolt across the bumpy field, strike into the back wood-road, and turn off upon an old stumpy track over which cord wood was carted years ago. Here in the hollow at the foot of a high wooded hill, the winds have whirled the oak and maple leaves into drifts almost knee-deep.

We are off the main road, far into the heart of the woods. We straddle stumps; bend down saplings; stop while the horse takes a bite of sweet birch; tack and tip and tumble and back through the tight squeezes between the trees; and finally, after a prodigious amount of whoa-ing and oh-ing and squealing and screeching, we land right side up and so headed that we can start the load out toward the open road.

AUTUMN

You can yell all you want to when you go leafing; yell at every stump you hit; yell every time a limb knocks off your hat or catches you under the chin; yell when the horse stops suddenly to browse on the twigs and stands you meekly on your head in the bottom of the rig. You can screech and howl and yell like the wild Indian that you are, you can dive and wrestle in the piles of leaves and cut all the crazy capers you know; for this is a Saturday, these are the wild woods and the noisy leaves, and who is there looking on besides the mocking jays and the crows?

The leaves pile up. The wind blows keen among the tall, naked trees; the dull cloud hangs low above the ridge; and through the cold gray of the maple swamp below you, peers the face of Winter.

You start up the ridge with your rake and draw down another pile, thinking, as you work, of the pig. The thought is pleasing. The warm glow all over your body strikes into your heart. You rake away as if it were your own bed you were gathering — as really it is. He that rakes for his pig, rakes also for himself. A merciful man is merciful to his beast; and he that gathers leaves for his pig spreads a blanket of down over his own winter bed.

Is it to warm my feet on winter nights that I pull on my boots at ten o'clock and go my round at the barn? Yet it warms my feet through and through to look into the stalls and see the cow chewing her cud, and the horse cleaning up his supper hay, standing to his fetlocks in his golden bed of new rye-straw; and then, going to the pig's pen, to hear him snoring louder than the north wind, somewhere in the depths of his leaf-bed, far out of sight. It warms my heart, too!

So the leaves pile up. How good a thing it is to have a pig to work for! What zest and purpose it lends to one's raking and piling and storing! If I could get nothing else to spend myself on, I should surely get me a pig. Then, when I went to walk in the woods, I should be obliged, occasionally, to carry a rake and a bag with me — much better things to take into the woods than empty hands, and sure to scratch into light a number of objects that would never come within the range of opera-glass or gun or walking stick. To see things through a twenty-four-toothed rake is to see them very close, as through a microscope magnifying twenty-four diameters.

And so, as the leaves pile up, we keep a sharp lookout for what the rake uncovers — here, under a rotten stump, a hatful of acorns, probably gathered by the white-footed wood mouse. For the stump gives at the touch of the rake, and a light kick topples it down the hill, spilling out a big nest of feathers and three dainty little creatures that scurry into the leaf-piles like streaks of daylight. They are the white-footed wood mice, long-tailed, big-eared, and as clean and high-bred looking as greyhounds.

Combing down the steep hillside with our rakes, we dislodge a large stone, exposing a black patch of fibrous roots and leaf mould, in which something moves and disappears. Scooping up a double handful of the mould, we capture a little red-backed salamander.

This is not the "red" salamander that Mr. Burroughs tells us is "the author of that fine plaintive piping to be heard more or less frequently, according to the weather, in our summer and autumn woods." His "red" salamander is really a "dull orange, variegated with minute specks or spots," a species I have never found here in my New England woods.

Nor have I ever suspected my red-backed salamander of piping; though he may do it, as may the angleworms, for aught I am able to hear, so filled with whir of iron wheels are my dull ears. But listen! Something piping! Above the rustle of the leaves we also hear a "fine plaintive" sound — no, a shrill and ringing little racket, rather, about the bigness of a penny whistle.

Dropping the rake, we cautiously follow up the call — it seems to speak out of every tree trunk — and find the piper clinging to a twig, no salamander at all, but a tiny tree-frog, Pickering's hyla, his little bagpipe blown almost to bursting as he tries to rally the scattered summer by his tiny, mighty "skirl." Take him nose and toes, he is surely as much as an inch long, not very large to pipe against the north wind turned loose in the leafless woods.

We go back to our raking. Above us, among the stones of the slope, hang bunches of Christmas fern; around the foot of the trees we uncover trailing clusters of gray-green partridge vine, glowing with crimson berries; we rake up the prince's pine, pipsissewa, creeping jennie, and wintergreen red with ripe berries, — a whole bouquet of evergreens, — exquisite, fairy-like forms, that later shall gladden our Christmas table.

But how they gladden and cheer the October woods! Summer dead? Hope all gone? Life vanished away? See here, under this big pine, a whole garden of arbutus, green and budded, almost ready to bloom! The snows shall come before their sweet eyes open; but open they will at the very first touch of spring. We will gather a few, and let them wake up in saucers of clean water in our sunny south windows.

Leaves for the pig, and arbutus for us! We make a clean sweep down the hillside, "jumping" a rabbit from its form, or bed, under a brush-pile; discovering where a partridge roosts in a low-spreading hemlock; coming upon a snail cemetery, in a hollow hickory stump; turning up a yellow-jacket's nest, built two-thirds underground; tracing the tunnel of a bob-tailed mouse in its purposeless windings in the leaf mould; digging into a woodchuck's —

"But come, boys, get after those bags! It is leaves in the hay-rig that we want, not woodchucks at the bottom of woodchuck holes." Two small boys catch up a bag and hold it open, while the third boy stuffs in the crackling leaves. Then I come along with my big feet and pack the leaves in tight, and onto the rig goes the bulging thing!

AUTUMN

Exciting? If you can't believe it exciting, hop up on the load and let us jog you home. Swish! bang! thump! tip! turn! joggle! jolt! — Hold on to your ribs! Look out for the stump! Isn't it fun to go leafing? Isn't it fun to do anything that your heart does with you — even though you do it for a pig?

Just watch the pig as we shake out the bags of leaves. See him caper, spin on his toes, shake himself, and curl his tail. That curl is his laugh. We double up and weep when we laugh hard; but the pig can't weep, and he can't double himself up, so he doubles up his tail. There is where his laugh comes off, curling and kinking in little spasms of pure pig joy!

Boosh! Boosh! he snorts, and darts around the pen like a whirlwind, scattering the leaves in forty ways, to stop short — the shortest stop! — and fall to rooting for acorns.

He was once a long-tusked boar of the forest, — this snow-white, sawed-off, pug-faced little porker of mine — ages and ages ago. But he still remembers the smell of the forest leaves; he still knows the taste of the acorn-mast; he is still wild pig in his soul.

And we were once long-haired, strong-limbed savages who roamed the forest hunting him — ages and ages ago. And we, too, like him, remember the smell of the fallen leaves, and the taste of the forest fruits — and of pig, *roast* pig! And if the pig in his heart is still a wild boar, no less are we, at times, wild savages in our hearts.

Anyhow, for one day in the fall I want to go "leafing." I want to give my pig a taste of acorns, and a big pile of leaves to dive so deep into that he cannot see his pen. I can feel the joy of it myself. No, I do not live in a pen; but then, I might, if once in a while I did not go leafing, did not escape now and then from my little daily round into the wide, wild woods — my ancestral home.

A CHAPTER OF THINGS TO HEAR THIS FALL

I

You ought to hear the scream of the hen-hawks circling high in the air. In August and September and late into October, if you listen in the open country, you will hear their piercing whistle, — shrill, exultant *scream* comes nearer to describing it, — as they sail and sail a mile away in the sky.

II

You ought to go out upon some mowing hill or field of stubble and hear the crickets, then into the apple orchard and hear the katydids, then into the high grass and bushes along the fence and hear the whole stringed chorus of green grasshoppers, katydids, and crickets. You have heard them all your life; but the trouble is that, because you have heard them so constantly in the autumn, and because one player after another has come gradually into the orchestra, you have taken them as part of the natural course of things and have never really heard them individually, to know what parts they play. Now anybody can hear a lion roar, or a mule bray, or a loon laugh his wild crazy laugh over a silent mountain lake, and know what sound it is; but who can hear a cricket out of doors, or a grasshopper, and know which is which?

III

Did you ever hear a loon laugh? You ought to. I would go a hundred miles to hear that weird, meaningless, melancholy, maniacal laughter of the loon, or great northern diver, as the dusk comes down over some lonely lake in the wilderness of the far North. From Maine westward to northern Illinois you may listen for him in early autumn; then, when the migration begins, anywhere south to the Gulf of Mexico. You may never hear the call of the bull moose in the northern woods, nor the howl of a coyote on the western prairies, nor the wild *cac, cac, cac* of the soaring eagles, nor the husky *yap, yap, yap* of the fox. But, if you do, "make a note of it," as Captain Cuttle would say; for the tongues that utter this wild language are fast ceasing to speak to us.

IV

One strangely sweet, strangely wild voice that you still may hear in our old apple orchards, is the whimpering, whinnying voice of the little screech owl. "When night comes," says the bird book, "one may hear the screech owl's tremulous, wailing whistle. It is a weird, melancholy call, welcomed only by those who love Nature's voice, whatever be the medium through which she speaks." Now listen this autumn for the screech owl; listen until the weird, melancholy call *is* welcomed by you, until the shiver that creeps up your back turns off through your hair, as you hear the low plaintive voice speaking to you out of the hollow darkness, out of the softness and the silence of night.

V

You ought to hear the brown leaves rustling under your feet.

AUTUMN

"Heaped in the hollows of the grove, the autumn leaves lie dead;
They rustle to the eddying gust, and to the rabbit's tread."

And they should rustle to your tread as well. Scuff along in them where they lie in deep windrows by the side of the road; and hear them also, as the wind gathers them into a whirling flurry and sends them rattling over the fields.

VI

You ought to hear the cry of the blue jay and the caw of the crow in the autumn woods.

"The robin and the wren are flown, but from the shrub the jay,
and from the wood-top calls the crow through all the gloomy day."[6]

Everybody knows those lines of Bryant, because everybody has heard that loud scream of the jay in the lonesome woods, and the *caw, caw, caw* of the sentinel crow from the top of some tall tree. The robins may not be all gone, for I heard and saw a flock of them this year in January; but they are silent now, and so many of the birds have gone, and the woods have become so empty, that the cries of the jay and the crow seem, on a gloomy day, to be the only sounds in all the hollow woods. There could hardly be an autumn for me if I did not hear these two voices speaking — the one with a kind of warning in its shrill, half-plaintive cry; the other with a message slow and solemn, like the color of its sable coat.

---

[6] Both quotations are from William Cullen Bryant's "The Death of the Flowers."

AUTUMN

VII

You ought to hear, you ought to *catch*, I should say, a good round scolding from the red squirrel this fall. A red squirrel is always ready to scold you (and doubtless you are always in need of his scolding), but he is never so breathless and emphatic as in the fall. "Whose nuts are these in the woods?" he asks, as you come up with your stick and bag. "Who found this tree first? Come, get out of here! Get right back to the city and eat peanuts! Come, do you hear? Get out of this!"

No, don't be afraid; he won't "eat you alive" — though I think he might if he were big enough. He won't blow up, either, and burst! He is the kind of fire-cracker that you call a "sizzler" — all sputter and no explosion. But isn't he a tempest! Isn't he a whirlwind! Isn't he a red-coated cyclone! Let, him blow! The little scamp, he steals birds' eggs in the summer, they say; but there are none now for him to steal, and the woods are very empty. We need a dash of him on these autumn days, as we need a dash of spice in our food.

In the far western mountains he has a cousin called the Douglas squirrel; and Mr. John Muir calls him "the brightest of all the squirrels I have ever seen, a hot spark of life, making every tree tingle with his prickly toes, a condensed nugget of fresh mountain vigor and valor, as free from disease as a sunbeam. How he scolds, and what faces he makes, all eyes, teeth, and whiskers!"

You must hear him this fall and take your scolding, whether you deserve it or not.

VIII

You ought to hear in the cedars, pines, or spruces the small thin *cheep, cheep, cheep* of the chickadees or the kinglets. You

104

must take a quiet day on the very edge of winter and, in some
sunny dip or glade, hear them as they feed and flit about you.
They speak in a language different from that of the crow and
the jay. This tiny talk of the kinglet is all friendly and cheerful
and personal and confidential, as if you were one of the party
and liked spiders' eggs and sunshine and didn't care a snap for
the coming winter! In all the vast gray out of doors what bits
of winged bravery, what crumbs of feathered courage, they
seem! One is hardly ready for the winter until he has heard
them in the cedars and has been assured that they will stay, no
matter how it snows and blows.

IX

You ought to hear, some quiet day or moonlit night in
October or November, the baying of the hounds as they
course the swamps and meadows on the heels of the fox.
Strange advice, you say? No, not strange. It is a wild, fierce cry
that your fathers heard, and their fathers, and theirs — away
on back to the cave days, when life was hardly anything but
the hunt, and the dogs were the only tame animal, and the
most useful possession, man had. Their deep bass voices have
echoed through all the wild forests of our past, and stir within
us nowadays wild memories that are good for us again to
feel. Stand still, as the baying pack comes bringing the quarry
through the forest toward you. The blood will leap in your
veins, as the ringing cries lift and fall in the chorus that echoes
back from every hollow and hill around; and you will on with
the panting pack — will on in the fierce, wild exultation of the
chase; for instinctively we are hunters, just as all our ancestors
were.

No, don't be afraid. You won't catch the fox.

X

You ought to hear by day — or better, by night — the call of the migrating birds as they pass over, through the sky, on their way to the South. East or west, on the Alantic or on the Pacific shore, or in the vast valley of the Mississippi, you may hear at night, so high in air that you cannot see the birds, these voices of the passing migrants. *Chink, chink, chink!* will drop the calls of the bobolinks — fine, metallic, starry notes; *honk, honk, honk!* the clarion cry of the wild geese will ring along the aerial way, as they shout to one another and to you, listening far below them on the steadfast earth.

Far away, yonder in the starry vault, far beyond the reach of human eyes, a multitude of feathered folk, myriads of them, are streaming over; armies of them winging down the long highway of the sky from the frozen North, down to the rice fields of the Carolinas, down to the deep tangled jungles of the Amazon, down beyond the cold, cruel reach of winter.

Listen as they hail you from the sky.

HONK, HONK, HONK!

HONK, honk, honk! Out of the silence of the November night, down through the depths of the darkened sky, rang the thrilling call of the passing geese.

Honk, honk, honk! I was out of bed in an instant; but before I had touched the floor, there was a patter of feet in the boys' room, the creak of windows going up, and — silence.

Honk, honk, honk! A mighty flock was coming. The stars shone clear in the far blue; the trees stood dark on the rim of the North; and somewhere between the trees and the stars, somewhere along a pathway running north and south, close up against the distant sky, the wild geese were winging.

Honk, honk, honk! They were overhead. Clear as bugles, round and mellow as falling flute notes, ordered as the tramp of soldiers, fell the *honk, honk, honk*, as the flock in single line, or double like the letter V, swept over and was gone.

We had not seen them. Out of a sound sleep they had summoned us, out of beds with four wooden legs and no wings; and we had heard the wild sky-call, had heard and followed through our open windows, through the dark of the night, up into the blue vault under the light of the stars.

Round and dim swung the earth below us, hushed and asleep in the soft arms of the night. Hill and valley lay close together, farm-land and wood-land, all wrapped in the coverlet of the dark. City and town, like watch fires along the edge of a sleeping camp, burned bright on the rivers and brighter still on the ragged line of shore and sea, for we were far away near the stars. The mountains rose up, but they could not reach us; the white lakes beckoned, but they could not call us down. For the stars were bright, the sky-coast was clear, the wind in our wings was the keen, wild wind of the North, and the call that we heard — ah! who knows the call? Yet, who does not know

107

it — that distant haunting call to fly, fly, fly?

I found myself in my bed the next morning. I found the small boys in their beds. I found the big round sun in the sky that morning and not a star in sight! There was nothing unusual to be seen up there, nothing mysterious at all. But there was something unusual, something mysterious to be seen in the four small faces at the breakfast-table that morning — eyes all full of stars and deep with the far, dark depths of the midnight sky into which they had gazed — into which those four small boys had flown!

We had often heard the geese go over before, but never such a flock as this, never such wild waking clangor, so clear, so far away, so measured, swift, and — gone!

I love the sound of the ocean surf, the roar of a winter gale in the leafless woods, the sough of the moss-hung cypress in the dark southern swamps. But no other voice of Nature is so strangely, deeply thrilling to me as the *honk, honk, honk* of the passing geese.

For what other voice, heard nowadays, of beast or bird is so wild and free and far-resounding? Heard in the solemn silence of the night, the notes fall as from the stars, a faint and far-off salutation, like the call of sentinels down the picket line — "All's well! All's well!" Heard in the open day, when you can see the winged wedge splitting through the dull gray sky, the notes seem to cleave the dun clouds, driven down by the powerful wing-beats where the travelers are passing high and far beyond the reach of our guns.

The sight of the geese going over in the day, and the sound of their trumpetings, turn the whole world of cloud and sky into a wilderness, as wild and primeval a wilderness as that distant forest of the far Northwest where the howl of wolves is still heard by the trappers. Even that wilderness, however, is passing; and perhaps no one of us will ever hear the howl of wolves in the hollow snow-filled forests, as many of our parents have heard. But the *honk* of the wild geese going over we should all hear, and our children should hear; for this flock of wild creatures we have in our hands to preserve.

The wild geese breed in the low, wet marshes of the half-frozen North, where, for a thousand years to come they will not interfere with the needs of man. They pass over our northern and middle states and spend the winter in the rivers, marshes, and lagoons of the South, where, for another thousand years to come, they can do little, if any, harm to man, but rather good.

But North and South, and all along their journey, back and forth, they are shot for sport and food. For the wild geese cannot make this thousand-mile flight without coming down to rest and eat; and wherever that descent is made, there is pretty sure to be a man with a gun on the watch.

Here, close to my home, are four ponds; and around the sides of each of them are "goose blinds" — screens made of cedar and pine boughs fixed into the shore, behind which the gunners lie in wait. More than that, out upon the surface of the pond are geese swimming, but tied so that they cannot escape — geese that have been raised in captivity; and placed there to lure the flying wild flocks down. Others, known as "flyers," are kept within the blind to be let loose when a big flock is seen approaching — to fly out and mingle with them and decoy them to the pond. These "flyers" are usually young birds and, when thrown out upon their wings, naturally come back, bringing the wild flock with them, to their fellows fastened in the pond.

A weary flock comes winging over, hungry, and looking for a place to rest. Instantly the captive geese out on the pond see them and set up a loud honking. The flying flock hear them and begin to descend. Then they see one (tossed from the

109

blind) coming on to meet them, and they circle lower to the pond, only to fall before a fury of shots that pour from behind the blind.

Those of the flock that are not killed rise frightened and bewildered to fly to the opposite shore, where other guns riddle them, the whole flock sometimes perishing within the ring of fire!

Such shooting is a crime because it is unfair, giving the creature no chance to exercise his native wit and caution. The fun of hunting, as of any sport, is in playing the game — the danger, the exercise, the pitting of limb against limb, wit against wit, patience against patience; not in a heap of carcasses, the dead and bloody weight of mere meat!

If the hunter would only play fair with the wild goose, shoot him (the wild Canada goose) only along the North Carolina coast, where he passes the winter, then there would be no danger of the noble bird's becoming extinct. And the hunter then would know what real sport is, and what a long-headed, far-sighted goose the wild goose really is — for there are few birds with his cunning and alertness.

Along the Carolina shore the geese congregate in vast numbers; and when the day is calm, they ride out into the ocean after feeding, so far off shore that no hunter could approach them. At night they come in for shelter across the bars, sailing into the safety of the inlets and bays for a place to sleep. If the wind rises, and a storm blows up, then they must remain in the pools and water-holes, where the hunter has a chance to take them. Only here, where the odds, never even, are not all against the birds, should the wild geese be hunted.

With the coming of March there is a new note in the clamor of the flocks, a new restlessness in their movements; and, before the month is gone, many mated pairs of the birds have flocked together and are off on their far northern journey to the icy lakes of Newfoundland and the wild, bleak marshes of Labrador.

Honk, honk, honk! Shall I hear them going over, — going northward, — as I have heard them going southward this fall? Winter comes down in their wake. There is the clang of the cold in their trumpeting, the closing of iron gates, the bolting of iron doors for the long boreal night. They pass and leave the forests empty, the meadows brown and sodden, the rivers silent, the bays and lakes close sealed. Spring will come up with them on their return; their *honk, honk, honk* will waken the frogs from their oozy slumbers and stir every winter sleeper to the very circle of the Pole.

Honk, honk, honk! Oh, may I be awake to hear you, ye strong-winged travelers on the sky, when ye go over northward, calling the sleeping earth to waken, calling all the South to follow you through the broken ice-gates of the North!

Honk, honk, honk! The wild geese are passing — southward!

THE SEASON OF
WINTER

ROBERT BRUCE HORSFALL

HUNTING THE SNOW

You want no gun, no club, no game-bag, no steel trap, no snare when you go hunting the snow. Rubber boots or overshoes, a good, stout stick to help you up the ridges, a pair of field-glasses and a keen eye, are all you need for this hunt, — besides, of course, the snow and the open country.

You have shoveled the first snow of the winter; you have been snowballing in it; you have coasted on it; and gone sleigh-riding over it; but unless you have gone hunting over it you have missed the rarest, best sport that the first snowfall can bring you.

Of all the days to be out in the woods, the day that follows the first snowfall is — the best? No, not the best. For there is the day in April when you go after arbutus; and there is the day in June when the turtles come out to lay in the sand; the muggy, cloudy day in August when the perch are hungry for you in the creek; the hazy Indian Summer day when the chestnuts are dropping for you in the pastures; the keen, crisp February day when the ice spreads glassy-clear and smooth for you over the mill-pond; the muddy, raw, half-thawed, half-lighted, half-drowned March day when the pussy-willows are breaking, and the first spring frogs are piping to you from the meadow. Then there is — every day, every one of the three hundred and sixty-five days, each of them best days to be out in the live world of the fields and woods.

But *one* of the very best days to be out in the woods is the day that follows the first winter snowfall, for that is the day when you must shoulder a good stout stick and go gunning. Gunning with a stick? Yes, with a stick, and rubber boots, and bird-glasses. Along with this outfit you might take a small jointed foot-rule with which to measure your quarry, and a notebook to carry the game home in.

113

It ought to be the day after the first real snow, but not if that snow happens to be a blizzard and lies deep in dry powdery drifts, for then you could hardly follow a trail if you should find one. Do not try the hunt, either, if the snow comes heavy and wet; for then the animals will stay in their dens until the snow melts, knowing, as they do, that the soft slushy stuff will soon disappear. The snow you need will lie even and smooth, an inch or two deep, and will be just damp enough to pack into tight snowballs.

If, however, the early snows are not ideal, then wait until over an old crusted snow there falls a fresh layer about an inch deep. This may prove even better hunting, for by this time in the winter the animals and birds are quite used to snow-walking, and besides, their stores of food are now running short, compelling them to venture forth whether or not they wish to go.

It was early in December that our first hunting-snow came last year. We were ready for it, waiting for it, and when the winter sun broke over the ridge, we started the hunt at the hen-yard gate, where we saw tracks in the thin, new snow that led us up the ridge, and along its narrow back, to a hollow stump. Here the hunt began in earnest; for not until that trail of close, double, nail-pointed prints went under the stump were the four small boys convinced that we were tracking a skunk and not a cat.

The creature had moved leisurely — that you could tell by the closeness of the prints. Wide-apart tracks in the snow mean hurry. Now a cat, going as slowly as this creature went, would have put down her dainty feet almost in a single line, and would have left round, cushion-marked holes in the snow, not triangular, nail-pointed prints like these. Cats do not venture into holes under stumps, either.

We had bagged our first quarry! No, no! We had not pulled

that wood pussy out of his hole and put him into our game-bag. We did not want to do that. We really carried no bag; and if we had, we should not have put the wood pussy into it, for we were hunting tracks, not animals, and "bagging our quarry" meant trailing a creature to its den, or following its track till we had discovered something it had done, or what its business was, and why it was out. We were on the snow for animal *facts*, not pelts.

We were elated with our luck, for this stump was not five minutes by the ridge path from the hen-yard. And here, standing on the stump, we were only sixty minutes away from Boston Common by the automobile, driving no faster than the law allows. So we were hunting, not in a wilderness, but just outside our dooryard and almost within the borders of a great city.

And that is the first interesting fact of our morning hunt. No one but a lover of the woods and a careful walker on the snow would believe that here in the midst of hayfields, in sight of the smoke of city factories, so many of the original wild wood-folk still live and travel their night paths undisturbed.

Still, this is a rather rough bit of country, broken, ledgy, boulder-strewn, with swamps and woody hills that alternate with small towns and cultivated fields for many miles around.

Here the animals are still at home, as this hole of the skunk's under the stump proved. But there was more proof. As we topped the ridge on the trail of the skunk, we crossed another trail, made up of bunches of four prints, — two long and broad, two small and roundish, — spaced about a yard apart.

A hundred times, the winter before, we had tried that trail in the hope of finding the form or the burrow of its maker; but it crossed and turned and doubled, and always led us into a tangle, out of which we never got a clue. It was the track of the great northern hare, as we knew, and we were relieved to see the strong prints of our cunning neighbor again; for, what with the foxes and the hunters, we were afraid it might have fared ill with him. But here he was, with four good legs under him; and, after bagging our skunk, we returned to pick up the hare's trail, to try our luck once more.

We followed his long, leisurely leaps down the ridge, out into our mowing-field, and over to the birches below the house. Here he had capered about in the snow, had stood up on his haunches and gnawed the bark from off a green oak sucker two and a half feet from the ground. This, doubtless, was pretty near his length, stretched out — an interesting item; not exact to the inch, perhaps, but close enough for us; for who would care to kill him in order to measure him with scientific accuracy?

Nor was this all; for up the footpath through the birches came the marks of two dogs. They joined the marks of the hare. And then, back along the edge of the woods to the bushy ridge, we saw a pretty race.

It was all in our imaginations, all done for us by those long-flinging footprints in the snow. But we saw it all — the white hare, the yelling hounds, nip and tuck, in a burst of speed across the open field which must have left a gap in the wind behind.

It had all come as a surprise. The hounds had climbed he hill on the scent of a fox, and had started the hare unexpectedly. Off he had gone with a jump. But just such a jump of fear is what a hare's magnificent legs were intended for.

Those legs carried him a clear twelve feet in some of the longest leaps for the ridge; and they carried him to safety, so far as we could read the snow. In the medley of hare-and-hound tracks on the ridge there was no sign of a tragedy.

He had escaped again — but how and where we have still to learn.

We had bagged our hare, — yet we have him still to bag,

— and taking up the trail of one of the dogs, we continued our hunt. One of the joys of this snow-hunting is having a definite road or trail blazed for you by knowing, purposeful wild-animal feet.

You do not have to blunder ahead, breaking your way into this wilderness world, trusting luck to bring you somewhere. The wild animal or the dog goes this way, and not that, for a reason. You are watching that reason all along; you are pack-fellow to the hound; you hunt with him.

Here the hound had thrust his muzzle into a snowcapped pile of slashings, had gone clear round the pile, then continued on his way. But we stopped; for out of the pile, in a single, direct line, ran a number of mouse prints, going and coming. A dozen white-footed mice might have traveled that road since the day before, when the snow had ceased falling.

We entered the tiny road, for in this kind of hunting a mouse is as good as a mink, and found ourselves descending the woods toward the garden patch below.

Halfway down we came to a great red oak, into a hole at the base of which, as into the portal of some mighty castle, ran the road of the mice. That was the end of it. There was not a single straying footprint beyond the tree.

I reached in as far as my arm would go, and drew out a fist-ful of pop-corn cobs. So here was part of my scanty crop! I pushed in again, and gathered up a bunch of chestnut shells, hickory-nuts and several neatly rifled hazelnuts. This was story enough. There must be a family of mice living under the slash-ing pile, who for some good reason kept their stores here in the recesses of this ancient red oak. Or was this some squirrel's barn being pilfered by the mice, as my barn is the year round? It was not all plain. But this question, this constant riddle of the woods, is part of our constant joy in the woods. Life is always new, and always strange, and always fascinating.

WINTER

It has all been studied and classified according to species. Any one knowing the woods at all, would know that these were mouse tracks, would even know that they were the tracks of the white-footed mouse, and not the tracks of the jumping mouse, the house mouse, or the meadow mouse. But what is the whole small story of these prints? What purpose, what intention, what feeling, do they spell? What and why? — a hundred times!

So it is not the bare tracks that we are hunting; it is the meaning of the tracks where they are going, and what they are going for. Burns saw a little mouse run across the furrows as he was plowing and wrote a poem about it.[7] So could we write a poem if we like Burns would stop to think what the running of these little mice across the snow might mean. The woods and fields, summer and winter, are full of poems that might be written if we only knew just all that the tiny snow-prints of a wood mouse mean, or understood just what, "root and all, and all in all," the humblest flower is.

The pop-corn cobs, however, we did understand; they told a plain story; and, falling in with a gray squirrel's track not far from the red oak, we went on, our burdenless game-bag heavier, our hearts lighter that we, by the sweat of our brows, had contributed a few ears of corn to the comfort of this snowy winter world.

The squirrel's track wound up and down the hillside, wove in and out and round and round, hitting every possible tree, as if the only road for a squirrel was one that looped and doubled, and tied up every stump, and zigzagged into every tree trunk in the woods.

But all this maze was no ordinary journey. He had not run

---

[7] Robert Burns (1759-96), famed Scottish poet who wrote "To a Mouse."

this coil of a road for breakfast, because a squirrel, when he travels, say for distant nuts, goes as directly as you go to your school or office; only he goes not by streets, but by trees, never crossing more of the open in a single rush than the space between him and the nearest tree that will take him on his way.

What interested us here in the woods was the fact that a second series of tracks, just like the first, except that they were only about half as large, dogged the larger tracks persistently, leaping tree for tree, and landing track for track with astonishing accuracy — tracks which, had they not been evidently those of a smaller squirrel, would have read to us most menacingly.

As this was the mating season for squirrels, I suggested that it might have been a kind of Atalanta's race here in the woods. But why did so little a squirrel want to mate with one so large? They would not look well together, was the answer of the small boys. They thought it much more likely that Father Squirrel had been playing wood-tag with one of his children.

Then, suddenly, as sometimes happens in the woods, the true meaning of the signs was fairly hurled at us, for down the hill, squealing and panting, rushed a full-sized gray squirrel, with a red squirrel like a shadow, like a weasel, at his heels.

For just an instant I thought it was a weasel, so swift and silent and gliding were its movements, so set and cruel seemed its expression, so sure, so inevitable, its victory.

Whether it ever caught the gray squirrel or not and what it would have done had it caught the big fellow, I do not know. But I have seen the chase often — the gray squirrel nearly exhausted with fright and fatigue, the red squirrel hard after him. They tore round and round us, then up over the hill, and disappeared.

One of the rarest prints for most snow-hunters nowadays, but one of the commonest hereabouts, is the quick, sharp track of the fox. In the spring particularly, when my fancy young chickens are turned out to pasture, I have spells of fearing that the fox will never be exterminated here in this untillable but beautiful chicken country. In the winter, however, when I see Reynard's trail across my lawn, when I hear the music of the baying hounds and catch a glimpse of the white-tipped brush swinging serenely in advance of the coming pack, I cannot but admire the capable, cunning rascal, cannot but be glad for him, and marvel at him, so resourceful, so superior to his almost impossible conditions, his almost numberless foes.

We started across the meadow on his trail, but found it leading so straightaway for the ledges, and so continuously blotted out by the passing of the pack, that, striking the wallowy path of a muskrat in the middle of the meadow, we took up the new scent to see what the shuffling, cowering water-rat wanted from across the snow.

A man is known by the company he keeps, by the way he wears his hat, by the manner of his laugh; and among the wild animals nothing tells more of character than their manner of moving. You can read animal character as easily in the snow as you can read act and direction.

The timidity, the indecision, the lack of purpose, the restless, meaningless curiosity of this muskrat were evident from the first in the starting, stopping, returning, going-on track he had plowed out in the thin snow.

He did not know where he was going or what he was going for; he knew only that he insisted upon going back, but all the while kept going on; that he wanted to go to the right or to the left, yet kept moving straight ahead.

We came to a big wallow in the snow, where, in sudden fear, he had had a fit at the thought of something that might not have happened to him had he stayed at home. Every foot of the trail read, "He would if he could; if he couldn't, how could he?"

120

We followed him on, across a dozen other trails for it is not every winter night that the muskrat's feet get the better of his head, and, willy-nilly, take him abroad. Strange and fatal weakness! He goes and cannot stop.

Along the stone wall of the meadow we tracked him, across the highroad, over our garden, into the orchard, up the woody hill to the yard, back down the hill to the orchard, out into the garden, and back toward the orchard again; and here, on a knoll just at the edge of the scanty, skeleton shadow where the sunlight fell through the trees, we lost him.

Two mighty wings, we saw, had touched the snow lightly here, and the lumbering trail had vanished as into the air.

Close and mysterious the shadowy silent wings hang poised indoors and out. Laughter and tears are companions. Life begins, but death sometimes ends the trail. Yet the sum of life, outdoors and in, is peace, gladness, and fulfillment.

THE TURKEY DRIVE

The situation was serious enough for the two boys. It was not a large fortune, but it was their whole fortune, that straggled along the slushy road in the shape of five hundred weary, hungry turkeys, which were looking for a roosting-place.

But there was no place where they could roost, no safe place, as the boys well knew, for on each side of the old road stretched the forest trees, a dangerous, and in the weakened condition of the turkeys, an impossible roost on such a night as was coming.

For the warm south wind had again veered to the north; the slush was beginning to grow crusty, and a fine sifting of snow was slanting through the open trees. Although it was still early afternoon, the gloom of the night had already settled over the forest, and the turkeys, with empty crops, were peevishly searching the bare trees for a roost. It was a strange, slow procession that they made, here in the New Brunswick forest — the flock of five hundred turkeys, toled forward by a boy of eighteen, kept in line by a well-trained shepherd-dog that raced up and down the straggling column, and urged on in the rear by a boy of nineteen, who was followed, in his turn, by an old horse and farm wagon, creeping along behind.

It was growing more difficult all the time to keep the turkeys moving. But they must not be allowed to stop until darkness should put an end to the march. And they must not be allowed to take to the trees at all. Some of them, indeed, were too weak to roost high; but the flock would never move forward again if exposed in the tall trees on such a night as this promised to be.

The thing to do was to keep them stirring. Once allow them to halt, give one of them time to pick out a roosting-limb for himself, and the march would be over for that afternoon. The boys knew their flock. This was not their first drive. They knew from experience that once a turkey gets it into his small head to roost, he is bound to roost. Nothing will stop him. And in this matter the flock acts as a single bird.

In the last village, back along the road, through which they had passed, this very flock took a notion suddenly to go to roost, and to go to roost on a little chapel as the vesper bells were tolling. The bells were tolling, the worshipers were gathering, when, with a loud gobble, one of the turkeys in the flock sailed into the air and alighted upon the ridge-pole beside the belfry! Instantly the flock broke ranks, ran wildly round the little building, and with a clamor that drowned the vesper bell, came down on the chapel in a feathered congregation that covered every shingle of the roof. Only the humor and quick wit of the kindly old priest prevented the superstitious of his people from going into a panic. The service had to wait until the birds made themselves comfortable for the night — belfry, roof, window-sills, and porch steps thick with roosting turkeys!

The boys had come to have almost a fear of this mania for roosting, for they never knew when it might break out or what strange turn it might take. They knew now, as the snow and the gray dusk began to thicken in the woods, that the flock must not go to roost. Even the dog understood the signs, — the peevish *quint, quint, quint*, the sudden bolting of some gobbler into the brush, the stretching necks, the lagging steps, — and redoubled his efforts to keep the line from halting.

For two days the flock had been without food. Almost a week's supply of grain, enough to carry them through to the border, had been loaded into the wagon before starting in upon this wild, deserted road through the Black Creek region; but the heavy, day-long snowstorm had prevented their moving at all for one day, and had made travel so nearly impossible since then that here they were, facing a blizzard, with night upon them, five hundred starving turkeys straggling wearily before them, and a two days' drive yet to go!

The two brothers had got a short leave from college, and had started their turkey drive in the more settled regions back from the New Brunswick border. They had bought up the turkeys from farm to farm, had herded them in one great flock as they drove them leisurely along, and had moved all the while toward the state line, whence they planned to send them through Maine for the New England market. Upon reaching the railroad, they would rest and feed the birds, and ship them, in a special freight-car ordered in advance, to a Boston commission house, sell the horse and rig for what they could get and, with their dog, go directly back to college.

More money than they actually possessed had gone into the daring venture. But the drive had been more than successful until the beginning of the Black Creek road. The year before they had gone over the same route, which they had chosen because it was sparsely settled and because the prices were low. This year the farmers were expecting them; the turkeys were plentiful; and the traveling had been good until this early snow had caught them here in the backwoods and held them; and now, with the sudden shift of the wind again to the north, it threatened to delay them farther, past all chance of bringing a single turkey through alive.

But George and Herbert Totman had not worked their way into their junior year at college to sit down by the roadside while there was light to travel by. They were not the kind to let their turkeys go roost before sundown. It was a slow and solemn procession that moved through the woods, but it moved — toward a goal that they had set for that day's travel.

All day, at long intervals, as they had pushed along the deep forest road, the muffled rumble of distant trains had come to them through the silence; and now, although neither of them had mentioned it, they were determined to get out somewhere near the tracks before the night and the storm should settle down upon them. Their road, hardly more here than a wide trail, must cross the railroad tracks, as they remembered it, not more than two or three miles ahead.

Leaving more and more of the desolate forest behind them with every step, they plodded doggedly on. But there was so much of the same desolate forest still before them! Yet yonder, and not far way, was the narrow path of the iron track through the interminable waste; something human — the very sight of it enough to warm and cheer them. They would camp to-night where they could see a train go by.

The leaden sky lowered closer upon them. The storm had not yet got under full headway, but the fine icy flakes were flying faster, slanting farther, and the wind was beginning to drone through the trees. Without a halt, the flock moved on through the thickening storm. But the dog was having all that he could do to keep the stragglers in order; and George, in the rear, saw that they must stir the flock, for the birds were gradually falling back into a thick bunch before him.

Hurrying back to the wagon, he got two loaves of bread, and ran ahead with them to Herbert. The famished turkeys seemed to know what he carried, and broke into a run after him. For half a mile they kept up the gait, as both boys, trotting along the road, dropped pieces of bread on the snow.

Then the whole game had to be repeated; for the greater part of the flock, falling hopelessly behind, soon forgot what they were running after, and began to cry, "*Quint! quint! quint!*" — the roosting-cry! So, starting again in the rear with the bread George carried the last of the flock forward for another good run.

"We should win this game," Herbert panted, "if we only had loaves enough to make a few more touch-downs."

"There's half an hour yet to play," was George's answer.

"But what on?"

"Oh, on our nerve now," the older boy replied grimly.

"That railroad is not far ahead," said Herbert.

"Half an hour ahead. We've got to camp by that track to-night or —"

"Or what?"

But George had turned to help the dog head off some runaways.

Herbert, picking up a lump of frozen leaves and snow, began to break this in front of the flock to tole them on.

He had hardly started the birds again, when a long-legged gobbler brushed past him and went swinging down the road, calling, "*Quint! quint! quint!*" to the flock behind. The call was taken up and passed along the now extended line, which, breaking immediately into double-quick, went streaming, after him.

Herbert got out of the way to let them pass, too astonished for a moment to do more than watch them go. It was the roosting-cry! An old gobbler had given it; but as it was taking him, for once, in the right direction, Herbert ordered back the dog that had dashed forward to head him off, and fell in with George to help on the stragglers in the rear.

As the laggards were brought up to a slight rise in the road, the flock was seen a hundred yards ahead, gathered in a dark mass about a telegraph-pole! It could be nothing else, for through the whirling snow the big cross-arms stood out, dim but unmistakable.

It was this that the gobbler had spied and started for, this sawed and squared piece of timber, that had suggested a barnyard to him, — corn and roost, — as to the boys it meant a human presence in the forest and something like human companionship.

It was after four o'clock now, and the night was hard upon

them. The wind was strengthening every minute; the snow was coming finer and swifter. The boys' worst fears about the storm were beginning to be realized.

But the sight of the railroad track heartened them. The strong-armed poles, with their humming wires, reached out hands of hope to them; and getting among the turkeys, they began to hurry them off the track and down the steep embankment, which fortunately offered them here some slight protection from the wind. But as fast as they pushed the birds off, the one-minded things came back on the track. The whole flock, meanwhile, was scattering up and down the iron rails and settling calmly down upon them for the night.

They were going to roost upon the track! The railroad bank shelved down to the woods on each side, and along its whitened peak lay the two black rails like ridge-poles along the length of a long roof. In the thick half-light of the whirling snow, the turkeys seemed suddenly to find themselves at home: and as close together as they could crowd, with their breasts all to the storm, they arranged themselves in two long lines upon the steel rails.

And nothing could move them! As fast as one was tossed down the bank, up he came. Starting down the lines, the boys pushed and shoved to clear the track; but the lines re-formed behind them quickly, evenly, and almost without a sound. As well try to sweep back the waves of the sea! They worked together to collect a small band of the birds and drive them into the edge of the woods; but every time the band dwindled to a single turkey that dodged between their legs toward its place on the roost. The two boys could have kept *two* turkeys off the rails, but not five hundred.

"The game is up, George," said Herbert, as the sickening thought of a passing train swept over him. The words were hardly uttered when there came the *tankle, tankle* of the big cow-bell hanging from the collar of the horse, that was just now coming up to the crossing!

George caught his breath and started over to stop the horse, when, above the loud hum of the wires and the sound of the wind in the forest trees, they heard through the storm the muffled whistle of a locomotive.

"Quick! The horse, Herbert! Hitch him to a tree and come!" called George, as he dived into the wagon and pulled out their lantern. "Those birds could wreck the train!" he shouted, and hurried forward along the track with his lighted lantern in his hand.

It was not the thought of the turkeys, but the thought of the people on the flying Montreal express, — if that it was, — that sped him up the track. In his imagination he saw the wreck of a ditched train below him; the moans of a hundred mangled beings he heard sounding in his ears!

On into the teeth of the blinding storm he raced, while he strained his eyes for a glimpse of the coming train.

The track seemed to lie straightaway in front of him, and he bent his head for a moment before the wind, when, out of the smother of the snow, the flaring headlight leaped almost upon him.

He sprang aside, stumbled, and pitched headlong down the bank, as the engine of a freight, with a roar that dazed him, swept past.

But the engineer had seen him, and there was a screaming of iron brakes, a crashing of cars together, and a long-drawn shrieking of wheels, as the heavy train slid along the slippery rails to a stop.

As the engineer swung down from his cab, he was met, to his great astonishment, by a dozen turkeys clambering up the embankment toward him. He had plowed his way well among the roosting flock and brushed them unhurt from the rails as the engine skidded along to its slow stop.

By this time the conductor and the train-hands had run forward to see what it all meant, and stood looking at the strange obstruction on the track, when Herbert came into the glare of the headlight and joined them. Then George came panting up, and the boys tried to explain the situation. But their explanation only made a case of sheer negligence out of what at first had seemed a mystery to the trainmen. Both the engineer and the conductor were anxious and surly. Their train was already an hour late; there was a through express behind, and the track must be cleared at once.

And they fell at once to clearing it conductor, fireman, brakemen, and the two boys. Those railroad men had never tried to clear a track of roosting turkeys before. They cleared it, a little of it, but it would not stay cleared, for the turkeys slipped through their hands, squeezed between their legs, ducked about their heels, and got back into place. Finally the conductor, putting two men in line on each rail, ordered the engineer to follow slowly, close upon their heels, with the train, as they scattered the birds before them.

The boys had not once thought of themselves. They had had no time to think of anything but the danger and the delay that they had caused. They helped with all their might to get the train through, and as they worked, silently listened to the repeated threats of the conductor.

At last, with a muttered something, the conductor kicked one of the turkeys into a fluttering heap beneath the engine, and, turning, commanded his crew to stand aside and let the engineer finish the rest of the flock.

The men got away from the track. Then, catching Herbert by the arm, George pointed along the train, and bending, made a tossing motion toward the top of the cars.

"Quick!" he whispered. "One on every car!" and stepping

calmly back in front of the engine, he went down the opposite side of the long train.

As he passed the tender, he seized a big gobbler, and sent him with a wild throw up to the top of a low coal-car, just as Herbert, on his side, sent another fluttering up to the same perch. Both birds landed with a flap and a gobble that were heard by the other turkeys up and down the length of the train. Instantly came a chorus of answering gobbles as every turkey along the track saw, in the failing light, that real buildings — farmyard buildings — were here to roost on! And into the air they went, helped all along the train by the two boys, who were tossing them into the cars, or upon the loads of lumber, as fast as they could pass from car to car. Luckily, the rails were sleety, and the mighty driving-wheels, spinning on the ice with their long load, which seemed to freeze continually to the track, made headway so slowly that the whole flock had come to roost upon the cars before the train was fairly moving.

Conductor and brakeman, hurrying back to board the caboose, were midway of the train before they noticed what was happening. *How* it was happening they did not see at all, so hidden were the movements of the two boys in the swirl of the blinding snow. For just an instant the conductor checked himself. But it was too late to do anything. The train was moving, and he must keep it moving as fast as he could to the freight-yards ahead at the junction — the very yards where, even now, an empty car was waiting for the overdue turkeys.

As he ran on down the track and swung aboard the caboose, two other figures closed in behind the train. One of them, seizing the other by the arm, landed him safe upon the steps, and then shouted at him through the storm: —

"Certainly you shall! I'm safe enough! I'll drive on to that old sawmill to-night. Feed 'em in the morning and wait for me! Good-by," and as the wind carried his voice away, George

Totman found himself staring after a ghost-white car that had vanished in the storm.

He was alone; but the thought of the great flock speeding on to the town ahead was company enough. Besides, he had too much to do, and to do quickly, to think of himself; for the snow was blocking his road, and the cold was getting at him. But how the wires overhead sang to him! How the sounding forest sang to him as he went back to give the horse a snatch of supper!

He was soon on the road, where the wind at his back and the tall trees gave him protection. The four-wheeled wagon pulled hard through the piling snow, but the horse had had an easy day, and George kept him going until, toward eight o'clock, he drew up behind a lofty pile of slabs and sawdust at the old mill.

A wilder storm never filled the resounding forests of the North. The old mill was far from being proof against the fine, icy snow; but when George rolled himself in his heavy blanket and lay down beside his dog, it was to go to sleep to the comfortable munching of the horse, and with the thought that Herbert and the turkeys were safe.

And they were safe. It was late in the afternoon the next day when George, having left the wagon at the mill, came floundering behind the horse through the unbroken road into the streets of the junction, to find Herbert anxiously waiting for him, and the turkeys, with full crops, trying hard to go to roost inside their double-decked car.

A CHAPTER OF THINGS TO SEE THIS WINTER

I

The first snowstorm! I would not miss seeing the first snowstorm, not if I had to climb up to my high, tarry, smoky roof in the city and lie down on my back, as I once did, in order to shut out everything but the gray wavering flakes that came scattering from the sky. But how marvelously white and airy they looked, too, coming down over the blackened city of roofs, transfiguring it with their floating veil of purity! You must see the first snowfall, and, if you want to, jump and caper with the flakes, as I always do.

II

The sorrows of winter are its storms. They are its greatest glories also. One should no more miss the sight of the winter storms than he should miss the sight of the winter birds and stars, the winter suns and moons! A storm in summer is only an incident; in winter it is an event, a part of the main design. Nature gives herself over by the month to the planning and bringing off of the winter storms — vast arctic shows, the dreams of her wildest moods, the work of her mightiest minions. Do not miss the soft feathery fall that plumes the trees and that roofs the sheds with Carrara marble; the howling blizzard with its fine cutting blast that whirls into smoking crests; the ice-storm that comes as slow, soft rain to freeze as it falls, turning all the world to crystal: these are some of the miracles of winter that you must not fail to see.

III

You must see how close you had passed to and fro all summer to the vireo's nest, hanging from the fork on a branch of some low bush or tree, so near to the path that it almost brushed your hat. Yet you never saw it! Go on and make a study of the empty nests; see particularly how many of them were built out along the roads or paths, as if the builders wished to be near their human neighbors — as, indeed, I believe they do. Study how the different birds build — materials, shapes, finish, supports; for winter is the better season in which to make such study, the summer being so crowded with interests of its own.

IV

When the snow hardens, especially after a strong wind, go out to see what you can find in the wind furrows of the snow in the holes, hollows, pockets, and in footprints in the snow. Nothing? Look again, closely — that dust — wind-sweepings — seeds! Yes, seeds. Gather several small boxes of them and when you return home take a small magnifying glass and make them out — the sticktights, gray birches, yellow birches, pines, ragweeds, milfoil — I cannot number them! It is a lesson in the way the winds and the snows help to plant the earth. Last winter I followed for some distance the deep frozen tracks of a fox, picking out the various seeds that had drifted into every footprint, just so far apart, as if planted in the snow by some modern planting-machine. It was very interesting.

V

When the snow lies five or six inches deep, walk out along the fence-rows, roadsides, and old fields to see the juncos, the sparrows, and goldfinches feeding upon the seeds of the dead weeds standing stiff and brown above the snow. Does the sight mean anything to you? What does it mean?

VI

Burns has a fine poem beginning[8] —

> "When biting Boreas, fell and doure,
> Sharp shivers thro' the leafless bow'r,"

in which, he asks, —

> "Ilk happing bird — wee, helpless thing! —
> . . . .
> what comes o' thee?
> Whare wilt thou cow'r thy chittering wing,
> An' close thy e'e?

Did you ever ask yourself the question? Go forth, then, as the dusk begins to fall one of these chill winter days and try to see "what comes o' " the birds, where they sleep these winter nights. You will find an account of my own watching in a chapter called "Birds' Winter Beds" in "Wild Life Near Home."

VII

You will come back from your watching in the dusk with the feeling that a winter night for the birds is unspeakably dreary, perilous, and chill. You will close the door on the darkness outside with a shiver as much from dread as from the cold.

---

[8] Robert Burns, "A Winter Night."

WINTER

"List'ning the doors an' winnocks rattle," —

You will think of the partridge beneath the snow, the crow in his swaying pine-top, the kinglet in the close-armed cedar, the wild duck riding out the storm in his freezing water-hole, and you will be glad for our four thick walls and downy blankets, and you will wonder how any creature can live through the long, long night of cold and dark and storm. But there is another view of this same picture; another picture, rather, of this same stormy, bitter night which you must not miss seeing. Go out to see how the animals sleep, what beds they have, what covers to keep off the cold: the mice in the corn-shocks; the muskrats in their thick mud homes; the red squirrels in their rocking, wind-swung beds, so soft; with cedar bark and so warm that never a tooth of the cold can bite through!

> "I heard nae mair, for Chanticleer
>   Shook off the pouthery snaw,
> And hail'd the morning with a cheer,
>   A cottage-rousing craw."

VIII

This winter I have had two letters asking me how best to study the mosses and lichens, and I answered, "Begin now." Winter, when the leaves are off, the ground bare, the birds and flowers gone, and all is reduced to singleness and simplicity — winter is the time to observe the shapes, colors, varieties, and growth of the lichens. Not that every lover of nature needs to know the long Latin names (and many of these lesser plants have no other names), but that every lover of the out-of-doors should notice them — the part they play in the color of things, the place they hold in the scheme of things, their exquisite shapes and strange habits.

IX

You should see the brook, "bordered with sparkling frost-work . . . as gay as with its fringe of summer flowers." You should examine under a microscope the wonderful crystal form of the snowflakes — each flake shaped by an infinitely accurate hand according to a pattern that seems the perfection, the very poetry, of mechanical drawing.

X

What a world of gray days, waste lands, bare woods, and frozen waters there is to see! And you should see them — gray and bare and waste and frozen. But what is a frozen pond for if not to be skated on? and waste white lands, but to go sleighing over? and cold gray days, but so many opportunities to stay indoors with your good books?

See the winter bleak and cheerless as at times you will, and as at times you ought; still if you will look twice, and think as you look, you will see the fishermen on the ponds catch-ing pickerel through the ice — life swimming there under the frozen surface! You will see the bare empty woodland fresh budded to the tip of each tiny twig — life all over the trees thrust forward to catch the touch of spring! You will see the wide flinty fields thick sown with seeds — life, more life than the sun and the soil can feed, sleeping there under "the tender, sculpturesque, immaculate, warming, fertilizing snow"!

A FEBRUARY FRESHET

One of the very interesting events in my out-of-door year is the February freshet. Perhaps you call it the February *thaw*. That is all it could be called this year; and, in fact, a *thaw* is all that it ever is for me, nowadays, living, as I do, high and dry here, on Mullein Hill, above a sputtering little trout brook that could not have a freshet if it tried.

But Maurice River could have a freshet without trying.[9] Let the high south winds, the high tides, and the warm spring rains come on together, let them drive in hard for a day and a night, as I have known them to do, and the deep, dark river goes mad! The tossing tide sweeps over the wharves, swirls about the piles of the great bridge, leaps foaming into the air, and up and down its long high banks beats with all its wild might to break through into the fertile meadows below.

There are wider rivers, and other, more exciting things, than spring freshets; but there were not when I was a boy. Why, Maurice River was so wide that there was but a single boy in the town, as I remember, who could stand at one end of the draw-bridge and skim an oyster-shell over to the opposite end! The best that I could do was to throw my voice across and hear it echo from the long, hollow barn on the other bank. It would seem to me to strike the barn in the middle, leap from end to end like a creature caged, and then bound back to me faint and frightened from across the dark tide.

I feared the river. Oh, but I loved it, too. Its tides were always rising or falling — going down to the Delaware Bay and

---

[9] Mullein Hill, with its summit 141 feet above sea level, is located in Plymouth County, Massachusetts, about 20 miles southeast of Boston. The Maurice River, in Cumberland County, New Jersey, flows into the Delaware Bay.

on to the sea. And in from the bay, or out to the bay, with white sails set, the big boats were always moving. And when they had gone, out over the wide water the gulls or the fish hawks would sail, or a great blue heron, with wings like the fans of an old Dutch mill, would beat ponderously across.

I loved the river. I loved the sound of the calking-maul and the adze in the shipyard, and the smell of the chips and tarred oakum; the chatter of the wrens among the reeds and calamus; the pink of the mallow and wild roses along the high mud banks; the fishy ditches with their deep sluiceways through the bank into the river; and the vast, vast tide-marshes that, to this day, seem to me to stretch way to the very edge of the world.

What a world for a boy to drive cows into every morning and drive them home from every night, as I used to help do! or to trap muskrats in during the winter; to go fishing in during the summer; to go splashing up and down in when the great February freshet came on!

For of all the events of the year, none had such fascination for me as the high winds and warm downpour that flooded the wharves, that drove the men of the village out to guard the river-banks, and that drowned out of their burrows and winter hiding-places all the wild things that lived within reach of the spreading tide.

The water would pour over the meadows and run far back into the swamps and farm lands, setting everything afloat that could float — rails, logs, branches; upon which, as chance offered, some struggling creature would crawl, and drift away to safety.

But not always to safety; for over the meadows the crows and fish hawks, gulls, herons, bitterns, and at night the owls, were constantly beating to pounce upon the helpless voyagers, even taking the muskrats an easy prey, through their weakness from exposure and long swimming in the water.

There would be only two shores to this wild meadow-sea —
the river-bank, a mere line of earth drawn through the water,
and the distant shore of the upland. If the wind blew from the
upland toward the bank, then the drift would all set that way,
and before long a multitude of shipwrecked creatures would
be tossed upon this narrow breakwater, that stood, a bare three
feet of clay, against the wilder river-sea beyond.

To walk up and down the bank then was like entering a
natural history museum where all the specimens were alive;
or like going to a small menagerie. Sparrows, finches, robins,
mice, moles, voles, shrews, snakes, turtles, squirrels, muskrats,
with even a mink and an opossum now and then, would scurry from beneath your feet or dive back into the water as you
passed along.

And by what strange craft they sometimes came! I once saw
two muskrats and a gray squirrel floating along on the top of one
of the muskrats' houses. And again a little bob-tailed meadow
mouse came rocking along in a drifting catbird's nest which the
waves had washed from its anchorage in the rosebushes. And
out on the top of some tall stake, or up among the limbs of
a tree you would see little huddled bunches of fur, a muskrat
perhaps that had never climbed before in his life, waiting, like
a sailor lashed to the rigging, to be taken off.

But it was not the multitude of wild things — birds, beasts,
insects — that fascinated me most, that led me out along the
slippery, dangerous bank through the swirling storm; it was
rather the fear and confusion of the animals, the wild giant-

spirit raging over the face of the earth and sky, daunting and terrifying them, that drew me.

Many of the small creatures had been wakened by the flood out of their deep winter sleep, and, dazed and numbed and frightened, they seemed to know nothing, to care for nothing but the touch of the solid earth to their feet.

All of their natural desires and instincts, their hatreds, hungers, terrors, were sunk beneath the waters. They had lost their wits, like human creatures in a panic, and, struggling, fighting for a foothold, they did not notice me unless I made at them, and then only took to the water a moment to escape the instant peril.

The sight was strange, as if this were another planet and not our orderly, peaceful world at all. Nor, indeed, was it; for fear cowered everywhere, in all the things that were of the earth, as over the earth and everything upon it raged the fury of river and sky.

The frail mud bank trembled under the beating of the waves; the sunken sluices strangled and shook deep down through the whirlpools sucking at their mouths; the flocks of scattered sea-birds — ducks and brant — veered into sight, dashed down toward the white waters or drove over with mad speed, while the winds screamed and the sky hung black like a torn and flapping sail.

And I, too, would have to drop upon all fours, with the mice and muskrats, and cling to the bank for my life, as the snarling river, leaping at me, would plunge clear over into the meadow below.

A winter blizzard is more deadly, but not more fearful, nor so wild and tumultuous. For in such a storm as this the foundations of the deep seem to be broken up, the frame of the world shaken, and you, and the mice, and the muskrats, share alike the wild, fierce spirit and the fear.

To be out in such a storm, out where you can feel its full fury, as upon a strip of bank in the midst of the churning waters, is good for one. To experience a common peril with your fellow mortals, though they be only mice and muskrats, is good for one; for it is to share by so much in their humble lives, and by so much to live outside of one's own little self.

And then again, we are so accustomed to the order and fair weather of our part of the globe, that we get to feel as if the universe were being particularly managed for us; nay, that we, personally, are managing the universe. To flatten out on a quaking ridge of earth or be blown into the river; to hear no voice but the roar of the storm, and to have no part or power in the mighty tumult of such a storm, makes one feel about the size of a mouse, makes one feel how vast is the universe, and how fearful the vortex of its warring forces!

The shriek of those winds is still in my ears, the sting of the driving rains still on my face, the motion of that frail mud bank, swimming like a long sea-serpent in the swirling waters, I can still feel to my finger-tips. And the growl of the river, the streaming shreds of the sky, the confusion beneath and about me, the mice and muskrats clinging with me for a foothold — I live it all again at the first spatter of a February rain upon my face.

To be out in a February freshet, out in a big spring break-up, is to get a breaking up one's self, a preparation, like Nature's, for a new lease of life — for spring.

A BREACH IN THE BANK

The February freshet had come. We had been expecting it, but no one along Maurice River had ever seen so wild and warm and ominous a spring storm as this. So sudden and complete a break-up of winter no one could remember; nor so high a tide, so rain-thick and driving a south wind. It had begun the night before, and now, along near noon, the river and meadows were a tumult of white waters, with the gale so strong that one could hardly hold his own on the drawbridge that groaned from pier to pier in the grip of the maddened storm.

It was into the teeth of this gale that a small boy dressed in large yellow "oil-skins" made his slow way out along the narrow bank of the river toward the sluices that controlled the tides of the great meadows.

The boy was *in* the large yellow oil-skins; not dressed, no, for he was simply inside of them, his feet and hands and the top of his head having managed to work their way out. It seems, at least, that his head was partly out, for on the top of the oil-skins sat a large black sou'wester. And in the arms of the oil-skins lay an old army musket, so big and long that it seemed to be walking away with the oil-skins, as the oil-skins seemed to be walking away with the boy.

I can feel the kick of that old musket yet, and the prick of the dried sand-burs among which she knocked me. I can hear the rough rasping of the chafing legs of those oil-skins too, though I was not the boy this time inside of them. But I knew the boy who was, a real boy; and I know that he made his careful way along the trembling river-bank out into the sunken meadows, meadows that later on I saw the river burst into and claim — and it still claims them, as I saw only last summer, when after thirty years of absence I once more stood at the end of that bank looking over a watery waste which was once

142

the richest of farm lands.

Never, it seemed, had the village known such wind and rain and such a tide. It was a strange, wild scene from the drawbridge — wharves obliterated, river white with flying spume and tossing ice-cakes, the great bridge swaying and shrieking in the wind, and over everything the blur of the swirling rain.

The little figure in yellow oil-skins was not the only one that had gone along the bank since morning, for a party of men had carefully inspected every foot of the bank to the last sluice, for fear that there might be a weak spot somewhere. Let a breach occur with such a tide as this and it could never be stopped.

And now, somewhat past noon, the men were again upon the bank. As they neared Five-Forks sluice, the central and largest of the water-gates, they heard a smothered *boom* above the scream of the wind in their ears. They were startled; but it was only the sound of a gun somewhere off in the meadow. It was the gun of the boy in the oil-skins.

Late that afternoon Doctor "Sam," driving home along the flooded road of the low back swamp, caught sight, as he came out in view of the river, of a little figure in yellow oil-skins away out on the meadow.

The doctor stopped his horse and hallooed. But the boy did not hear. The rain on his coat, the wind and the river in his ears drowned every other sound.

The dusk was falling, and as the doctor looked out over the wild scene, he put his hands to his mouth and called again. The yellow figure had been blotted out by the rain. There was no response, and the doctor drove on.

Meanwhile the boy in the yellow oil-skins was splashing slowly back along the narrow, slippery clay bank. He was wet, but he was warm, and he loved the roar of the wind and the beat of the driving rain.

143

As the mist and rain were fast mixing with the dusk of the twilight, he quickened his steps. His path in places was hardly a foot wide, covered with rose and elder bushes mostly; but bare in spots where holes and low worn stretches had been recently built up with cubes of the tough blue mud of the flats.

The tide was already even with the top of the bank and was still rising. It leaped and hit at his feet as he picked his way along. The cakes of white ice crunched and heeled up against the bank with here and there one flung fairly across his path. The tossing water frequently splashed across. Twice he jumped places where the tide was running over down into the meadows below.

How quickly the night had come! It was dark when he reached Five-Forks sluice — the middle point in the long, high bank. While still some distance off he heard the sullen roar of the big sluice, through which the swollen river was trying to force its way.

He paused to listen a moment. He knew the peculiar voice of every one of these gateways, as he knew every foot of the river-bank.

There was nothing wrong with the sullen roar. But how deep and threatening! He could *feel* the sound even better than he could hear it, far down below him. He started forward, to pass on, when he half felt, through the long, regular throbbing of the sluice, a shorter, faster, closer quiver, as of a small running stream in the bank very near his feet.

Dropping quickly to his knees, he laid his ear to the wet earth. A cold, black hand seemed to seize upon him. He heard the purr of running water!

It must be down about three feet. He could distinctly feel it tearing through.

Without rising he scrambled down the meadow side of the bank to see the size of the breach. He could hear nothing

144

of it for the boiling at the gates of the sluice. It was so dark he could scarcely see. But near the bottom the mud suddenly caved beneath his feet, and a rush of cold water caught at his knees.

The hole was greater than he feared.

Crawling back to the top of the bank, he leaned out over the river side. A large cake of ice hung in water in front of him. He pushed it aside and, bending until his face barely cleared the surface of the river, he discovered a small sucking eddy, whose swirling hole he knew ran into the breach.

He edged farther out and reached down under the water and touched the upper rim of the hole. How large might it be? Swinging round, he dug his fingers into the bank and lowered himself feet first until he stood in the hole. It was the size of a small bucket, but he could almost feel it going beneath his feet, and a sudden terror took hold upon him.

He was only a boy, and the dark night, the wild river, the vast, sweeping storm, the roar and tremor and tumult flattened him for a moment to the ridge of the bank in a panic of fear! But he heard the water running, he felt the bank going directly beneath where he lay, and getting to his feet he started for the village. A single hasty step and, but for the piles of the sluice, he would have plunged into the river.

He must feel his way; but he never could do it in time to save the bank. The breach must be stopped at once. He must stop it and keep it stopped until the next patrol brought help.

Feeling his way back, he dropped again upon his hands and knees above the breach to think for moment. The cake of ice hung as before in the eddy. Catching it, he tipped it and thrust it down across the mouth of the hole, but it slipped from his cold fingers and dived away. He pushed down the butt of his musket, turned it flat, but it was not broad enough to cover the opening. Then he lowered himself again, and stood in it, wedging the musket in between his boots; but he could feel the water still tearing through at the sides, and eating all the faster.

He clambered back to the top of the bank, put his hand to his mouth and shouted. The only answer was the scream of the wind and the cry of a brant passing overhead.

Then the boy laughed. "Easy enough," he muttered, and, picking up the musket, he leaned once more out over the river and thrust the steel barrel of the gun hard into the mud just below the hole. Then, stepping easily down, he sat squarely into the breach, the gun like a stake in front of him sticking up between his knees.

Then he laughed again, as he caught his breath, for he had squeezed into the hole like a stopper into a bottle, his big oil-skins filling the breach completely.

The water stood above the middle of his breast, and the tide was still rising. Darkness had now settled, but the ghostly ice-cakes, tipping, slipping toward him, were spectral white. He had to shove them back as now and then one rose before his face. The sky was black, and the deep water below him was blacker. And how cold it was!

Doctor Sam had been stopped by the flooded roads on his way home, and lights shone in the windows as he entered the village. He turned a little out of his way and halted in front of a small cottage near the bridge.

"Is Joe here?" he asked.

"No," answered the mother; "he went down the meadow for muskrats and has not returned yet. He's probably over with the men at the store."

Doctor Sam drove on to the store.

There was no boy in yellow oil-skins in the store.

Doctor Sam picked up a lighted lantern.

"Come on," he said. "I'm wet, but I want a look at those

146

sluices," and started for the river, followed immediately by the men, whom he led in single file out along the bank.

Swinging his lantern low, he pushed into the teeth of the gale at a pace that left the line of lights straggling far behind.

"What a night!" he growled. "If I had a boy of my own —" and he threw the light as far as he could over the seething river and then down over the flooded meadow.

Ahead he heard the roar of Five-Forks sluice, and swung his lantern high, as if to signal it, so like the rush of a coming train was the sound of the waters. But the little engineer in yellow oil-skins could not see the signal. He had almost ceased to watch. With his arm cramped about his gun, he was still at his post; but the ice-cakes floated in and touched him; the water no longer felt cold.

On this side, then on that, out over the swollen river, down into the tossing meadow flared the lantern as the doctor worked his way along.

Above the great sluice he paused a moment, then bent his head to the wind and started on, when his foot touched something soft that yielded strangely, sending a shiver over him, and his light fell upon a bunch of four dead muskrats lying in the path.

Along the meadow side flashed the lantern, up and over the riverside, and Doctor Sam, reaching quickly down, drew a limp little form in yellow oil-skins out of the water, as the men behind him came up.

A gurgle, a hiss, a small whirlpool sucking at the surface, — and the tide was again tearing through the breach that the boy had filled.

The men sprang quickly to their task, and did it well, while Doctor Sam, shielding the limp little form from the wind, forced a vial of something between the white lips, saying over to himself as he watched the closed eyes open, "If I had a boy of my own — If I had a boy —"

.   .   .   .

No, Doctor Sam never had a boy of his own; but he always felt, I think, that the boy of those yellow oil-skins was somehow pretty nearly his.

.   .   .   .

After a long, cold winter how I love the spatter on my face of the first February rain! The little trout brook below me foams and sometimes overruns the road, and as its small noise ascends the hill, I can hear — the wind on a great river, the wash of waves against a narrow bank, and the muffled roar of quaking sluices as when a February freshet is on.

THE LAST DAY OF WINTER

According to the almanac March 21st is the last day of winter. The almanac is not always to be trusted — not for hay weather, or picnic weather, or sailing weather; but you can always trust it for March 21st weather. Whatever the weather man at Washington predicts about it, whatever comes, — snow, sleet, slush, rain, wind, or frogs and sunshine, — March 21st is the last day of winter.

The sun "crosses the line" that day; spring crosses with him; and I cross over with the spring.

Let it snow! I have had winter enough. Let the wind rage! It cannot turn back the sun; it cannot blow away the "equinoctial line"; it cannot snow under my determination to have done, here and now, with winter!

The sun crosses to my side of the Equator on the 21st of March; there is nothing in the universe that can stop him. I cross over the line with him; and there is nothing under the sun that can stop me. When you want it to be spring, if you have the sun on your side of the line you can have spring. Hitching your wagon to a star is a very great help in getting along; but having the big sun behind you —

> "When descends on the Atlantic
>   The gigantic
> Storm-wind of the equinox"

is a tremendous help in ridding you of a slow and, by this time, wearisome winter, storm-wind and all.

Almanacs are not much to trust in; but if ever you prize one, it is on the 21st of March, — that is, if you chance to live in New England. Yet you can get along without the almanac — even in New England. Hang it up under the corner of the kitchen mantelpiece and come out with me into the March mud. We are going to find the signs of spring, the proofs that this is the last day of winter, that the sun is somewhere in the heavens and on *this* side of the equatorial line.

Almanac or no, and with all other signs snowed under, there are still our bones! Spring is in our bones. I cannot tell you how it gets into them, nor describe precisely how it feels. But, then, I do not need to. For you feel it in *your* bones too — a light, hollow feeling, as if your bones were birds' bones, and as if you could flap your arms and fly!

Only that you feel it more in your feet; and you will start and run, like the Jungle-folk, like Mowgli — run, run, run! Oh, it is good to have bones in your body, young bones with the "spring-running," in their joints, instead of the grit of rheumatism to stiffen and cripple you!

The roads are barely thawed. The raw wind is penetrating, and we need our greatcoats to keep out the cold. But look! A flock of robins — twenty of them, dashing into the cedars, their brown breasts plowing warm and red against the dull sky and the dark green of the trees! And wait — before we go down the hill — here behind the barn — no, there he dives from the telephone wire — Phœbe! He has just gotten back, and is simply killing time now (and insects too), waiting for Mrs. Phœbe to arrive, and housekeeping to begin.

Don't move! There in the gray clouds — two soaring, circling hen-hawks! *Kee-ee-you! Kee-ee-you!*

Round and round they go, their shrill, wild whistle piercing the four quarters of the sky and tingling down the cold spine of every forest tree and sapling, stirring their life blood until it seems to run red into their tops.

For see the maple swamp off yonder — the ashy gray of the boles, a cold steel-color two thirds of the way toward the top, but there changing into a faint garnet, a flush of warmth and life that seems almost to have come since morning!

Let us go on now, for I want to get some watercress from the brook — the first green growing thing for the table thus far! — and some pussy-willows for the same table, only not to eat. (There are many good things in this world that are not good to eat.) If the Sun were shining I should take you by way of the bee-hives to show you, dropping down before their open doors, a few eager bees bringing home baskets of pollen from the catkins of the hazelnut bushes. The hazelnut bushes are in bloom! Yes, in bloom! No, the skunk-cabbages are not out yet, nor the hepaticas, nor the arbutus; but the hazelnut bushes are in bloom, and — see here, under the rye straw that covers the strawberry-bed — a small spreading weed, green, and cheerily starred with tiny white flowers!

It is the 21st of March; the sun has crossed the line; the phœbes have returned; and here under the straw in the garden the chickweed, — *starwort* — first of the flowers, is in blossom!

But come on; I am not going back yet. This is the last day of winter. Cold? Yes, it is cold, raw, wretched, gloomy, with snow still in the woods, with frost still in the ground, and with not a frog or hyla anywhere to be heard. But come along. This is the last day of winter — of winter? No, no, it is the first day of spring. Robins back, phœbes back, watercress for the table, chickweed in blossom, and a bird's nest with eggs in it! Winter? Spring? Birds' eggs, did I say?

The almanac is mixed again. It always is. Who's Who in the Seasons when all of this is happening on the 21st of March? For here is the bird's nest with eggs in it, just as I said.

Watch the hole up under that stub of a limb while I tap on the trunk. How sound asleep! But I will wake them. *Rap-rap-rap!* There he comes — the big barred owl!

Climb up and take a peek at the eggs, but don't you dare to

touch them! Of course you will not. I need not have been so quick and severe in my command; for, if we of this generation do not know as much about some things as our fathers knew, we do at least know better than they that the owls are among our best friends and are to be most jealously protected.

Climb up, I say, and take a peek at those round white eggs, and tell me, Is it spring or winter? Is it the last day, or the first day, or the first and last in one? What a high mix-up is the weather — especially this New England sort!

But look at that! A snowflake! Yes, it is beginning to snow — with the sun crossing the line! It is beginning to snow, and down with the first flakes, like a bit of summer sky drops a bluebird, calling softly, sweetly, with notes that melt warm as sunshine into our hearts.

"For, lo, the winter is past, the rain is over and gone." But see how it snows! Yes, but see —

> The willows gleam with silver light;
>   The maples crimson glow —
> The first faint streaks on winter's east,
>   Far-off and low.
>
> The northward geese, with wingèd wedge,
>   Have split the frozen skies,
> And called the way for weaker wings,
>   Where midnight lies.
>
> Today a warm wind wakes the marsh;
>   I hear the hylas peep
> And o'er the pebbly ford, unbound,
>   The waters leap.
>
> The lambs bleat from the sheltered folds;
>   Low whispers spread the hills:

WINTER

The rustle of the spring's soft robes
    The forest fills.

The night, ah me! fierce flies the storm
    Across the dark dead wold;
The swift snow swirls; and silence falls
    On stream and fold.

All white and still lie stream and hill —
    The winter dread and drear!
Then from the skies a bluebird flies
    And — spring is here!

Other Works by Sharp

A Watcher in the Woods (1901)
Wild Life Near Home (1901)
Roof and Meadow (1904)
The Lay of the Land (1908)
The Face of the Fields (1911)
Where Rolls the Oregon (1914)
Beyond the Pasture Bars (1914)
The Whole Year Round (1915)
The Hills of Hingham (1916)
The Seer of Slabsides (1921)
Highlands and Hollows (1923)
The Magical Chance (1923)
The Spirit of the Hive: Contemplations of a Beekeeper (1925)
The Better Country (1928)

Colophon

Essays for this volume were selected from Dallas Lore Sharp's *The Whole Year Round*, reset and edited by Allison Shegda (Spring), Cuong Nguyen (Summer), Renee Fern (Autumn), and Stephen DeCicco (Winter). Renee Fern served as master editor for the entire volume. Publication was supervised by Tom Kinsella. Thanks to Paul W. Schopp and Mark Demitroff who suggested that Sharp's work was worth republishing.

The text is set in 11 point Garamond, with notes in 10 point. Pagination does not follow the original edition. Cover design suggested by Renee Fern and completed by Sarah Messina.

SJCHC

South Jersey Culture & History Center

www.ingramcontent.com/pod-product-compliance
Lightning Source LLC
Chambersburg PA
CBHW060900280326
41934CB00007B/1127